FORGET-ME-NOT

For centuries plants and flowers have been surrounded by their own unique legends, myths and folklore. Poets and playwrights since Elizabethan times have used them to convey sentiments in the subtlest of ways, but it was the Victorians who raised this symbolism to an art and for whom communicating in the Language of Flowers became a popular cult. Flowers were accorded a precise vocabulary, based largely on the floral language of the ancient Greek, Roman and Eastern cultures – and it was even possible to specify exact times and dates by the number and position of the leaves or buds on the stem of a plant. In an age of strict morals and repressed sexuality, the Language of Flowers served as a code between lovers and friends, who could quarrel, reproach, express grief, gratitude, admiration, love, pleasure, passion, indifference, friendship or sympathy, without ever inking their fingers.

Forget-Me-Not, which is arranged alphabetically by emotion, reveals many varied and intriguing meanings behind a host of plants and flowers, and explores their special powers and properties as well as the myths that surround them. On a practical level the book illustrates how to create a birthday posy tailor-made for its recipient and shows how to convey love in all its many guises.

FOLLY CAUSES GRIEF AND TEARS

FORGET-ME-NOT
A Floral Treasury

WRITTEN AND RESEARCHED BY
PAMELA TODD

ILLUSTRATED BY IAN PENNEY

Sentiments & Plant Lore from the
LANGUAGE of FLOWERS

A BULFINCH PRESS BOOK
LITTLE, BROWN AND COMPANY
BOSTON · TORONTO · LONDON

FOR
CHLOE, FLORENCE AND FREDERIC

AND
ELSIE

First Edition

ISBN 0-8212-2000-4

Library of Congress Catalog Card Number 92-54427
Library of Congress Cataloging-in-Publication information is available.

A CIP catalogue record for this book is available from the British Library.

Conceived, edited and designed by David Fordham.

Published simultaneously in the United States of America by Bulfinch Press,
an imprint and trademark of Little, Brown and Company (Inc.),
in Great Britain by Little, Brown and Company (UK) Ltd,
and in Canada by Little, Brown & Company (Canada) Limited

PRINTED AND BOUND IN GERMANY

CONTENTS

INTRODUCTION

"An exquisite invention this,
Worthy of Love's most honeyed kiss, –
This art of writing billet-doux
In buds and flowers, and bright hues!
In saying all one feels and thinks
In clever daffodils and pinks;
In puns of tulips, and in phrases,
Charming for their truth of daisies!"

JAMES HENRY LEIGH-HUNT

The language of flowers dates back to classical times: the term "poet laureate" comes from the Roman custom of crowning poets with laurel leaves; Cleopatra knew that roses spoke of love and a woman's beauty when she paid in gold coin to have the room in which she was to receive Mark Antony filled to a depth of two feet with rose petals. Elizabethan poets, too, were aware of the symbolism of flowers: "There's pansies," says Ophelia in Shakespeare's *Hamlet*, "that's for thoughts."

The oriental concept of the language of flowers was introduced to England by Lady Mary Wortley Montagu, wife of the ambassador to Constantinople, 1716-18. From this developed a European language of flowers which allowed for individual sentiments to be assigned – often arbitrarily and usually romantically – to individual flowers. In time, this practice caught the imagination of the Victorians to an extraordinary degree, for theirs was, in many ways, a sentimental age. Honour, courage and constancy were important manly virtues, while women were admired for their beauty, their maternal tenderness, purity and sweetness. Their place was in the home, tending to the needs of husband and family. Yet middle-class women, with servants to help run the

CONSOLATION ARISING FROM THOUGHTS
Snowdrops, the first brave and welcome flowers of spring, represent Consolation and arise from a highly decorative Victorian vase of pensive pansies, representing Thoughts.

house and look after the children, often found time weighed heavily on their hands. How should they fill their days? Needlework was encouraged, as was a little light reading, some music. Botany and flower-drawing were also deemed suitable occupations, particularly after a royal lead had been given by Queen Victoria and her daughters. "There is not a plant in the gardens of Kew," wrote Robert Thornton, "but has either been drawn by her gracious Majesty, or some of the princesses, with a grace and skill that reflects on these personages the highest honours." It is therefore not surprising that the language of flowers became ever more popular.

A tireless and often nostalgic preoccupation with the countryside, flowers and traditional, rural pursuits, combined with the sexual repressiveness of the time, encouraged a coy form of clandestine correspondence between surreptitious lovers. Courtship was a much longer, and probably more romantic, process than now and wild flowers, then unthreatened by intensive farming, grew in abundance. An intriguing means of expession was easily to hand if you understood the language.

Floral dictionaries, essential if a love affair was to thrive, proliferated. Since every flower had a meaning, carefully chosen posies served as eloquent, coded love letters. They could be delicate and subtle: mimosa epitomized the fashionable idea of a shy and bashful maiden. Or they could be more forthright: forget-me-nots appealed greatly to the Victorian sense of melodrama and high regard for blind, chaste devotion and were a constant favourite in bouquets and in cards and valentines.

However, the positioning and presentation of the flowers was crucial and mistakes could spell the end rather than the beginning of a relationship. A flower handed stem first, for example, would convey a meaning exactly the opposite of what the flower stood for: a rose-bud, with its thorns and leaves, says, "I fear, but I hope"; presented upside down, it means, "You must neither fear nor hope." The same rose-bud, stripped of its thorns, says "There is everything to hope for."; but stripped of its leaves, it says, "There is everything to fear."

For the men, flowers provided an eloquence they might themselves have lacked and for the women an (almost) innocent and certainly diverting method of communicating with members of the opposite sex. Poring over a bouquet of, say, broom, bluebells, a white water lily and rosemary, and decoding the message, "Your humility, constancy and purity of heart claim my affectionate remembrance", must have provided delicious enjoyment.

The rose, quite naturally, plays a leading role in the language of flowers, although the sentiment expressed depends on the colour. The white rose, employed as the symbol of silence when presented upright, says, "I am worthy of you", while a yellow rose signifies a waning of love.

Lovers grew fluent enough to manage dialogues, but even that was not enough. They needed a way of specifying date and time. Henry Phillips, in his *Floral Emblems* (1825), obliged them by devising a numbering system (reproduced below) and a singular method of distinguishing the days of the week.

> "Yet, no — not words, for they
> But half can tell love's feeling;
> Sweet flowers alone can say
> What passion fears revealing.
> A once bright roses's wither'd leaf,
> A tow'ring lily broken —
> Oh, these may pain a grief
> No words could e'er have spoken."
>
> THOMAS HOOD

Henry Phillips was a flower historian and friend of John Constable. *Floral Emblems*, one of eight charming and scholarly books he wrote, includes this system, entirely of his own devising, of 'leaflet numbers'. Since nature could not be expected to adapt to it readily, the system was employed more formally on painted cards, or embossed or engraved on commemorative china or plate.

"The numerical emblems are simply distinguished by the leaflets as far as eleven. From eleven to twenty they are denoted by berries added to leaf ten, as in the examples 12 to 15. Twenty to a hundred is represented by joining a compound leaf to the tenth, as in the example 20, which expresses two tens, and the odd number is formed by the addition of berries, as in the representation of 36, where three tens and six berries denote the number, and 77 is pictured in the same manner.

A hundred is represented on the same principal by ten tens, and which may be increased by a third leaflet and a branch of berries as far as 999, as the example 505. A thousand is distinguished by a frond of fern or brake to which a leaflet may be added to increase the number of thousands, in the same manner as the hundreds. Thus any given number may be explained, or the date of the year formed by foliage."

For those who became really practised in the art, sums of money could even be represented by using round leaflets to denote the pounds, oval the shillings and long pointed ones the pennies!

The system for signifying days of the week was equally singular. Individual leaves, usually of the lotus or water lily, were used to represent each day. Monday was a water lily leaf, exactly one half of which was light, the other dark; Tuesday a leaf divided into "the waters and the heavens, which are distinguished by one half being light, and the other blue or sea green". Wednesday's leaf was "divided into three colours, light for the heavens, blue for the waters, and green for the earth". Thursday was a green lotus leaf, plus flower; Friday a leaf plus insect. Saturday's leaf was filled with fruit and "the Sabbath day" was "distinguished by a simple olive leaf".

HE LOVES ME, HE LOVES ME NOT

"Twas the maiden's matchless beauty
That drew my heart a-nigh;
Not the fern-root potion
But the glance of her blue eye."

In affairs of the heart, flowers, leaves, plants and nuts have all been used to divine future husbands or confirm the fidelity of a lover. Many-petalled flowers like the daisy, dandelion and poppy, which lend themselves to the repetitive and random nature of the "he loves me, he loves me not" conundrum, are still popular today. No doubt the young girls who would wash their faces in the dew on May Day morning, hoping to become or remain beautiful, would also eagerly await Hallowe'en, for this was a particularly magical time – if they had not already seen the candlelit reflection of their future husband in the

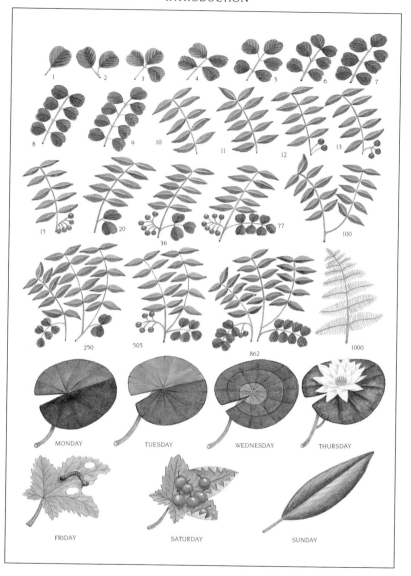

1 2 3 4 5 6 7

8 9 10 11 12 13

15 20 36 77 100

250 505 862 1000

MONDAY TUESDAY WEDNESDAY THURSDAY

FRIDAY SATURDAY SUNDAY

mirror, they could count on a line of hazelnuts to solve the riddle. These they would line up on a hot grate, giving each the name of a prospective husband. They would then recite, "If you love me pop and fly; if you hate me, burn and die." In another version, the nuts that cracked gave away the fickle suitors. To be doubly sure, a girl could throw the unbroken peel of an apple over her shoulder and then see what initial it formed. (Only advisable if you are in love with a Stephen, Simon or similar. Apple peel, however ingeniously cut, has difficulty arranging itself into a passable E or H.) A sentimental young girl was tireless in her search for a husband: a two- or four-leaf clover worn in the right shoe, for instance, would guarantee that the first man she met that day would be her husband, or that she would marry someone bearing the same name.

> "A clover, a clover of two,
> Put it in your right shoe;
> The first young man you meet,
> In field, street, or lane,
> You'll get him, or one of his name."

These charms and rites, although whimsical, existed the world over. Longfellow records the American colonists:

> "In the golden weather the Maize was husked, and the maidens
> Blushed at each blood-red ear, for that betokened a lover;
> But at the crooked laughed, and called it a thief in the cornfield:
> Even the blood-red ear to Evangeline brought not her lover."

And Goethe records Margaret in Faust:

> "And that scarlet poppies around like a bower,
> The maiden found her mystic flower.
> 'Now, gentle flower, I pray thee tell
> If my love loves, and loves me well;
> So may the fall of the morning dew
> Keep the sun from fading thy tender blue;
> Now I remember the leaves for my lot —
> He loves me not — he loves me — he loves me not —
> He loves me! Yes, the last leaf — yes!
> I'll pluck thee not for that last sweet guess;
> He loves me!' 'Yes,' a dear voice sighed;
> And her lover stands by Margaret's side."

Plants played their part, too, in love potions and philtres (in A *Midsummer Night's Dream*, Oberon tells Puck to place a pansy on the eyes of Titania, in order that, on awaking, she may fall in love with the first object she encounters). The root of the male fern was frequently used in love philtres and many plants gained an unlikely reputation as aphrodisiacs. Aristotle started the belief that mint was so powerful an aphrodisiac that people were warned to take it in moderation. Elizabethan rarities like potatoes and tomatoes (known as love apples) were also favourites.

The purslane, crocus and periwinkle were thought to inspire love; the myrtle not only created love, but preserved it. Moreover, flowers were used to check up on lovers during periods of separation: roses or lavender were hung on beds or hidden away in books and drawers and consulted later to show by their colour or freshness whether or not a lover had been true. Some plants could give direct access to an absent lover – it was said that by picking a slip of forget-me-not while thinking of your lover, he would immediately think of you. Poppies were also pressed into service: if a poppy petal placed in the palm made a snapping sound when hit with the fist then your lover was faithful.

GODS, WITCHES and FAIRIES

Plants have been worshipped, dedicated to the gods, used by, or to deter, witches, and some were thought to be the special province of fairies. Since classical times, there have been many myths and legends in which frightened nymphs, forsaken lovers and grieving gods were changed into flowers, plants or trees:

> "By this the boy that by her side lay killed
>   Was melted like a vapour from her sight;
> And in his blood that on the ground lay spilled
>   A purple flower sprang up, chequered with white,
> Resembling well his pale cheeks and the blood
> Which in round drops upon their whiteness stood."
>
> WILLIAM SHAKESPEARE

13

Numerous plants were associated with witches – vervain, rue, nightshade and monkshood were favourites – and as many more considered proof against them: cyclamen, angelica, pimpernel, to name a few. The three witches in *Macbeth* have a delicious time stirring their cauldron and tossing in "root of hemlock digg'd in the dark" and "slips of yew sliver'd in the moon's eclipse".

Fear of witchcraft was widespread, and when, for example, the butter would not set, or the cow fell ill, or someone died suddenly, it was a witch that was to blame. Witches were tricky characters, reputed to use fern-seed and hazelnuts to make themselves invisible or to appear in some disguise. A walnut placed under the chair of a suspected witch was said to make it impossible for her to rise. St John's wort or elder, the green juice of which, taken from the inner bark and anointed on the eyes of any baptized person, was said to render that person able to see witches. Elder was considered especially good at warding off witches, which explains why it is so often planted close to houses or stables.

> *"And I ha' been plucking plants among*
> *Hemlock, Henbane, Adder's tongue;*
> *Nightshade, Moonwort, Lizzard's bane,*
> *And twice, by the dogs, was like to be ta'en."*
>
> BEN JONSON

QUEEN VICTORIA
Born 24th May 1819

A regal birthday bouquet for Queen Victoria rising out of a vase composed of elm leaves, signifying Dignity; ash, Grandeur; and ivy, Marriage. The thornless rose symbolizes her Early Attachment to Albert; the rock rose her Popular Favour; blue violets, her favourite flower, Faithfulness; nasturtiums, Splendour and Patriotism; azalea, Temperance; tansy, Resistance; guelder rose, Winter or Age and the whole arrangement is topped by a crown imperial, symbolizing Majesty and Power.

Queen Victoria's birth date composed in ▶ leaves. The year is above, the day and month below.

Folklore is filled with tales of magic fairy rings of toadstool and wild thyme. Fairies, like witches, were said to avoid yellow flowers. Tulips served them as cradles in which to lull their fairy babies to sleep and foxgloves provided them with their clothes. The cowslip was once known as the fairy cup and Shakespeare describes Ariel reclining in "a cowslip's bell" and speaks of the small crimson drops in its blossom as "rubies, fairy favours".

> "I'll seek a four-legged clover
> In all the fairy dells,
> And if I find the charmed leaf,
> Oh, how I'll weave my spells!"

WEATHER LORE and HOROLOGICAL PLANTS

> "Mist in May, heat in June,
> Makes the harvest come right soon."

There is a great deal of weather lore attached to plants. Long before scientific weather-forecasting, plants were watched anxiously, for their blooming or otherwise was held to indicate particular conditions: for instance, when the bramble blossoms early in June an early harvest may be expected. Or:

> "If the oak is out before the ash,
> 'Twill be a summer of wet and splash;
> But if the ash is before the oak.
> 'Twill be a summer of fire and smoke."

Few farmers nowadays would sow seed by the moon, but it was once common practice and Thomas Tusser (for whom we have to thank for well-known aphorisms such as " 'Tis an ill wind that blows nobody any good", and "a fool and his money be soon at debate", advised in his *One Hundreth Pointes of Husbandrie*:

> *"Sow peas and beans in the wane of the moon,*
> *Who soweth them sooner, he soweth too soon,*
> *That they with the planet may rest and rise,*
> *And flourish with bearing, most plentiful wise."*

Other plants served shepherds and farm workers as clocks, since their petals could be counted on to open and close at specific times of day. The dandelion, for example, has been named the "peasant's clock" because its flowers open at 5 am and close in the evening during the summer, while its feathery seed-tufts have delighted children down the ages:

> *"Dandelion, with globe of down,*
> *The schoolboy's clock in every town,*
> *Which the truant puffs amain*
> *To conjure lost hours back again."*

The pimpernel was known as the shepherd's clock, and wild succory, creeping mallow, purple sandwort and smooth sow-thistle were also held to possess this horological ability.

THE DOCTRINE of SIGNATURES, FOLK MEDICINE and SIMPLES

The Doctrine of Signatures stems from a sixteenth-century medical theory which connected plant remedies with diseases. Most simply put, it stated that although God had visited man with disease and pestilence, He had also provided him with the cures. All he needed to do was to look around him.

William Coles, in his *Art of Simpling* (1656), describes it:

> *"Though sin and Satan have plunged mankind into an ocean of*
> *infirmities, yet the mercy of God which is over all His workes,*
> *maketh grasse to growe upon the mountains and herbes for the*
> *use of men, and hath not only stamped upon them a distinct*
> *forme, but also given them particular signatures, whereby a man*
> *may read even in legible characters the use of them."*

In some cases the plant which cured a disease also, conveniently, re-sembled it: scabious, for example, with its scabby appearance, was thought good for scabies; the spotted leaves of pulmonaria or lung-wort were a remedy for tubercular lungs; plants with a yellow sap would cure jaundice, and the crinkly walnut, bearing the whole 'signa-ture' of the head, was clearly good for disorders of the brain.

Simples, or folk remedies, were very popular forms of medicine and herbalists were people

> "Who knew the cause of everie maladie,
> Were it of colde or hotte, or moist or drie."

Nicholas Culpeper highly recommended mistletoe as "good for the grief of the sinew, itch, sores, and toothache, the biting of mad dogs and venomous beasts". Mandrake was said to cure infertility and Shakespeare speaks of it as an opiate. When reading William Coles' *The Art of Simpling*, one is struck by how little has changed. Nowadays women pay huge sums to cosmetic firms for anti-ageing creams; in times past they used to soak wild tansy in buttermilk for nine days to "make the complexion very fair", or request lady's-mantle, which was supposed to have the power of "restoring feminine beauty, however faded, to its early freshness".

JANE AUSTEN
Born 16th December 1776

Jane Austen's Eloquence has been celebrated by the yellow irises in her birthday bouquet, her Talent by the white pinks and her Honesty by the honesty seeds. Evoking some of her most loved books, we have added ama-ryllis for Pride and hibiscus for Persuasion — and her most loved heroines with the white lilies for Purity and Modesty, the red fuchsia for Taste, the lady's mantle for Fashion and the pot leek for Vivacity. The whole arrange-ment is bound with mint leaves symbolizing Virtue.

◀ *Jane Austen's birth date composed in leaves.*

FLOWERS and the CALENDAR

This is not a comprehensive monthly guide to flowers – that would fill a book of its own – but, since certain flowers are associated with specific dates, often saints' feast days, these have been picked out as they may help to make a birthday bouquet special.

January is a lean month for new flowers and the evergreen laurustinus (*Viburnum tinus*), with its clusters of pink and white flowers, is a welcome sight. It is dedicated to St Faine (January 1), an Irish abbess in the sixth century, and may be seen in bloom:

> *"Whether the weather be snow or rain,*
> *We are sure to see the flower of St Faine;*
> *Rain comes but seldom and often snow,*
> *And yet the viburnum is sure to blow."*

In the woodlands and hedgerows, winter heliotrope and winter aconite can be seen, as can the Christmas rose (*Helleborus niger*), dedicated to St Agnes (January 21), a Roman martyr who died in 304 AD when she was little more than a child.

> *"Over the land freckled with snow half-thawed*
> *The speculating rooks at their nests cawed*
> *And saw from elm-tops, delicate as flower of grass,*
> *What we below could not see, Winter pass."*
>
> EDWARD THOMAS

The little white snowdrop, which so delights and enchants us, has been named the fair maid of February and is associated with Candlemas Day (February 2). The primrose is dedicated to St Agatha

(February 13) and the welcome crocus, which also bursts into bloom about the middle of the month, is dedicated to St Valentine (February 14). With luck, the first violets, Queen Victoria's favourite flower, may also appear about now.

"The boys are up the woods with day
To fetch the daffodils away,
And home at noonday from the hills
They bring no dearth of daffodils."

A. E. HOUSEMAN

The patron saints of Wales and Ireland are celebrated in March: the leek is associated with St David (March 1), the shamrock with St Patrick (March 17). Then there's St Euphrasia (March 13), to whom the pansy is dedicated; St Edward (March 18), the crown imperial; and St Benedict (March 21), valerian. For many, however, the true flower of the spring equinox (March 21) is the exquisite wood anemone or windflower.

Yellow is March's colour: daffodils, buttercups, wallflowers, colts-foot and celandine are in their glory by the end of the month. The daffodil is also known as the Lent Lily, for it is particularly associated with the period, as is tansy (dedicated to St Athanasius, May 2), which was used to flavour special Lenten cakes.

Palm branches, yew and box are associated with Palm Sunday, which is also called Fig-Sunday, from an old custom of eating figs on that day. Good Friday was the appropriate day for sowing parsley seeds, cutting hazel rods for divining and hanging wreaths of elder over doors and windows to ward off lightning. The pasque flower, now sadly very rare, is also an Easter flower.

"And fairey month of waking mirth
From whom our joys ensue
Thou early gladder of the earth
Thrice welcom here anew."

JOHN CLARE

In April and May, according to John Gerard, "the cuckoo doth begin to sing her pleasant notes without stammering", and the arum, or cuckoo-pint, and ladysmock, often called cuckoo-flower, are in evidence. Orchids, primroses and cowslips brighten the roadsides and the blossom bursts into life on the fruit trees. The woods are full of bluebells, or harebells, dedicted to St George (April 23).

> "On St George's Day, when blue is worn,
> The blue harebells the fields adorn."

> "My wild field catalogue of flowers
> Grows in my rhymes as thick as showers
> Tedious and long as they may be
> To some, they never weary me.

JOHN CLARE

May is a glorious month for flowers: forget-me-nots, geraniums, columbine, cow parsley to name just a few. The hedgerows are festooned with hawthorn, known as May-bloom or May-tree. Lilac is also known as May-flower and lily-of-the-valley as May-lily.

SARAH BERNHARDT
Born 22nd October 1844

The French born actress Sarah Bernhardt's Strength of Character is signified by the gladioli in her birthday bouquet, her Female Ambition by the double narcissus, her Variety by the rosa mundi (she achieved distinction as a painter - signified by the auricula — as well as an actress and theatre manager.) The clematis signifies the Artifice of the stage, the black poplar her Courage in continuing to give performances at the front during the First World War despite having a leg amputated in 1915, and the vase of beech leaves symbolizes her Grandeur.

Sarah Bernhardt's birth date composed in ▶ leaves.

Flowers have played a large part in the traditional May Day (May 1) festival, when pagan ceremonies were performed to symbolize the turning cycle of the year and to usher in summer. Both old and young would go 'a-Maying' soon after midnight, breaking down branches from the trees and decorating them with garlands of flowers. On returning home soon after sunrise, they would then place their garlands over doors and windows. Shakespeare refers to the custom in *Henry VIII*:

> *"Tis as much impossible,*
> *Unless we sweep them from the doors with cannons,*
> *To scatter 'em, as 'tis to make 'em sleep*
> *On May Day morning."*

Various plants are associated with Whitsuntide. The peony is known as the Pentecost rose and Chaucer recommends:

> *"Have hatte of floures fresh as May,*
> *Chapelett of roses of Whitsunday,*
> *For sich array he costeth but lite."*

May 29 is Oak Apple Day, when gilded oak galls were worn to commemorate the Restoration of Charles II in 1660.

> *"Now summer is in flower and natures hum*
> *Is never silent round her sultry bloom."*
> JOHN CLARE

June is named after Juno, the wife of Jupiter, making it a queen of months, and it is therefore fitting that it should boast the queen of flowers – the rose. Roses, lavender, woodruff and box were once traditionally used to decorate churches on St Barnabus' Day (June 11), said to be the time for the start of hay-making.

> *"On St Barnabus'*
> *Put the scythe to the grass."*

Ragged Robin, too, is dedicated to St Barnabus; sweet william to St William (June 25) and parsley and pinks to St Peter (June 29). It was customary to sow turnip seed on June 17, the feast of St Botolph, hence the saint became familiarly and affectionately known as "the old turnip man".

The major pagan festival of the year falls on Midsummer's Eve (June 23), St John's Day. There were a great many superstitions attached to the day and many flowers dedicated to St John, including fennel and St John's wort, which used to be hung over doors of houses, along with green birch or pine and white lilies as a charm against witchcraft.

> "The scarlet lychnis, the garden's pride,
> Flames at St John the Baptist's tyde."
> AN EARLY CALENDAR OF ENGLISH FLOWERS

There was an old belief that a single kernel eaten each day from a pine cone collected from the top of a pine tree on St John's Day would make the person invulnerable to gun shot.

> "The breeze is stopt the lazy bough
> Hath not a leaf that dances now
> The totter grass upon the hill
> And spiders threads is hanging still
> The feathers dropt from morehens wing
> Which to the waters surface clings
> Are stedfast and as heavy seem
> As stones beneath them in the stream."
> JOHN CLARE

July is high summer, when the splash of red poppies is seen against the golden wheat and flowers are everywhere in profusion. Speedwell is dedicated to St Veronica (July 12); the daisy to St Margaret (July 20); and chicory to St James, who shares his feast day – July 25 – with St Christopher, to whom fleabane, meadowsweet, vetch and the royal fern are all dedicated. Another saint's day falls in July, St Swithin's (July 15), of which it was said:

> "St Swithin's Day, if thou dost rain,
> For forty days it will remain;
> St Swithin's Day, if thou be fair,
> For forty days 'twill rain nae mair."

August, heralding autumn, is harvest time and brings a few new arrivals: eyebright, devil's bit scabious, marjoram and vervain. The sunflower has been called St Bartholomew's (July 24) star, and it was said:

> "If St Bartholomew's Day be bright and clear
> Then a prosperous autumn comes that year."

> Thus harvest ends its busy reign
> And leaves the fields their peace again
> Where autumns shadows idly muse
> And tinge the trees with many hues."
>   JOHN CLARE

September is the month of berries: bramble, rowan, hawthorn, blackberry. elder. The michaelmas daisy is dedicated to St Michael the Archangel (September 29), as is angelica, and it was said that if acorns fall on St Michael's Day, there would be a bitter winter. The golden star lily is known as St Jerome's lily (September 30).

FLORENCE NIGHTINGALE
Born 12th May 1820

Florence Nightingale's Patience is symbolized by the vase of dock leaves, her Hospitality and Bravery by the acorns and oak leaves, her Consolation by the snowdrops and the red poppies, and her Perfect Goodness by the strawberries. Sickness is represented by the wood anemone and Life by the lucerne. Her Resolution is carried by the purple columbine and her Comfort by the scarlet geranium.

◀ *Florence Nightingale's birth date composed in leaves.*

26

"The green elm with the one great bough of bold
Lets leaves into the grass slip, one by one, —
The short hill grass, the mushrooms small, milk-white,
Harebell and scabious and tormentil,
That blackberry and gorse, in dew and sun,
Bow down to; and the wind travels too light
To shake the fallen birch leaves from the fern."

EDWARD THOMAS

October is the month of harvest festivals. The colours begin to change and for Keats it was the "season of mists and mellow fruitfulness". Chestnuts were traditionally eaten on St Simon's Day (October 28), and roses are particularly associated with the young Carmelite nun, St Therese of Lisieux (October 30). The last day of October, Hallowe'en, the day when the spirits of the dead were supposed to appear, was a symbolic day for love charms and divinations.

"In midnights of November
When Dead Man's Fair is nigh,
And danger in the valley,
And anger in the sky."

A. E. HOUSEMAN

November, ushered in by All Saints' Day (November 1), is the ebb of the flowering year. Wood sorrel is dedicated to St Cecilia (November 22) and love-in-a-mist to St Catherine (November 25).

"O! The holly and the ivy
Now that they are both full blown
Of all the trees that are in the wood
The holly bears the crown."

December is the month of the principal evergreens: the fir, ivy, laurel, bay, rosemary, holly and mistletoe, the traditional Christmas symbol.

An Early Calendar of English Flowers:

"The Snowdrop, in purest white arraie,
First rears her hedde on Candlemas daie;
While the Crocus hastens to the shrine
Of Primrose love on S. Valentine.
Then comes the Daffodil, beside
Our Ladye's Smock at our Ladye-tide.
Aboute S. George, when blue is worn,
The blue-Harebells the fields adorn;
Against the day of Holie Cross,
The Crowfoot gilds the flowerie grasse.
When S. Barnabie bright smiles night and daie,
Poor Ragged Robin blossoms in the haie.
The Scarlet Lychnis, the garden's pride,
Flames at S. John the Baptist's tide.
From Visitation to S. Swithin's showers,
The Lillie White reigns Queen of the Floures:
And Poppies, a sanguine mantle spred
For the blood of the Dragon S. Margaret shed.
Then under the wanton Rose, agen,
That blushes for Penitent Magdalen,
Till Lammas daie, called August's Wheel,
When the long Corn stinks of Camamile.
When Mary left us here belowe,
The Virgin's Bower is full in blow;
And yet anon, the full Sunflowre blew,
And became a starre for Bartholomew.
The Passion-floure long has blowed,
To betoken us signs of the Holy Roode.
The Michaelmas Daisies, among dede weeds,
Blooms for S. Michael's valourous deedes;
And seems the last of floures that stode,
Till the feste of S. Simon and S. Jude –
Save Mushrooms, and the Fungus race,
That grow till All-Hallow-tide takes place.
Soon the evergreen Laurel alone is greene,
When Catherine crownes all learned menne.
The Ivie and Holly Berries are seen,
And Yule Log and Wassaile come round agen."

The LANGUAGE of FLOWERS

A t first glance, some floral meanings may prove puzzling. Why should basil, such an excellent and popular herb, mean Hatred? The merry marigold, Despair? What association is there between the walnut and Intellect? Or the passion flower with Religious Superstition? But delve deeper and the connection clicks into place – in most instances. Some, like the olive with Peace or the rose with Beauty, are obvious. That the stinging nettle should stand for Cruelty in the language of flowers is unsurprising, but why should lobelia signify Malevolence or cress Stability? Some stubborn meanings resist decoding and must be put down to Victorian whimsicality. But most are illuminating and provide us with a fresh language as varied as our own moods.

> 'By all those token flowers, that tell,
> What words can never speak so well.'
> LORD BYRON

EMILY DICKINSON
Born 10th December 1830

The American poet Emily Dickinson's Love of Nature is represented by the magnolia and her Poetry by the sweet briar or eglantine. She never married and became a recluse after her love for the Reverend Charles Wadsworth was unrequited. (This Unfortunate or Hopeless Love is represented by scabious and yellow tulips – red carnations plead 'Alas for my poor heart.') She did, however, cultivate an intellectual Friendship with him, signified by the acacia leaves and the dog roses testify to the Pleasure and Pain this must have afforded her.

Emily Dickinson's birth date composed in ▶ *leaves.*

ABSENCE
WORMWOOD — *Artemisia absinthium*

"She was wean'd; I had then laid
Wormwood to my breast."
WILLIAM SHAKESPEARE

Poets allude to the "bitterness of absence". The extreme bitterness of all parts of the wormwood plant caused an "absence" of insects, and sprays of it used to be hung in cottages to drive them away:

"Where chamber is sweeped, and Wormwood is throwne,
No flea for his life dare abide to be known."

Also called St John's herb or St John's girdle, it was one of seven magical ingredients in a garland made on St John's Eve, which, designed to drive away demons and evil spirits, included other plants and leaves, as well as birds' claws. John Gerard recommended it, mixed with vinegar, as a good antidote for poisoning from mushrooms and toadstools.

AN ACCOMMODATING DISPOSITION
VALERIAN — *Valeriana officinalis*

Also known as bouncing Betty, blessed herb, capon's tail, kiss-me-quick, good neighbour, charity and finger grass, valerian was considered a mystic herb in pagan times and used in potions and philtres. Cats are attracted to its strong scent, as are rats, which have been trapped by using pieces of the root as bait. Indeed, the Pied Piper of Hamelin is said to have had the root concealed in his pocket. Medicinally the plant acts as a powerful sedative and so great was the faith in the plant among rural workers, it was also known as poor-man's-remedy and all-heal. It signifies an accommodating disposition because it was thought to be able to reconcile and restore affection between man and wife. In the fourteenth century, would-be pugilists were given valerian juice with the result, it was said, that peace was restored immediately. It is dedicated to St Benedict. In astrology, valerian falls under the rule of Mercury.

ACTIVITY

Thyme — *Thymus*

"O'er fringed heaths, wide lawns, and mountain steeps,
With silent step the artful Thyma creeps,
Unfolds with fragrant bloom her purple flow'rs,
And leads with frolic hand the circling hours."

Frances Arabella Rowden

Thyme was first made emblem of activity by the Greeks, who observed that its perfume stimulates the brain and excites the appetite. Bees seek it with great "activity" and the Greeks and Romans grew vast areas of it specifically for honey. This had a very distinctive flavour and the best, which came from Mount Hymettus near Athens, was famous for its delicious, sweet taste. Thyme also signified courage, style and elegance and "to smell of Thyme" was a term of high praise. It was the most fashionable scent among Athenian and, later, Roman men, who used it to perfume their chests after bathing. Medieval ladies embroidered sprays of thyme, with a bee, on scarves for their knights, as the emblem of courage and action. Thyme was a great favourite with Francis Bacon, who, in his plan for the perfect garden, directed the planting of paths with thyme and other herbs which, when trodden upon, would perfume the air "most delightfully". Herbalists recommended it to melancholics to "renew the spirit", and fairies and elves were reputed to be specially fond of wild thyme. In Shakespeare's *A Midsummer Night's Dream*, Oberon exclaims with delight:

"I know a bank whereon the Wild Thyme blows,
Where Oxlips and the nodding Violet grows,
Quite over-canopied with lush Woodbine.
With sweet Musk-Roses and with Eglantine."

However, to bring a sprig of shepherd's thyme, as wild thyme is called, into the house was thought to be very unlucky, as by doing so you would bring death or severe illness to a member of your family.

"For he painted the things that matter,
The tints that we all pass by;
Like the little blue wreaths of incense
That the wild thyme breathes to the sky."

Alfred Noyes

AFFLICTION

A L O E — *Succotrine aloe* and Aloe vera

"The woful teris that thei letin fal
As bittir werin, out of teris kinde,
For paine, as is ligne aloes, or gal."
GEOFFREY CHAUCER

The Victorians became very enthusiastic about this giant plant, which is found mainly in arid lands, particularly South Africa, and built hothouses to accommodate great quantities of them in England. They have long been associated with grief and sorrow: the Arabic name for aloe, *saber*, means patience and aloes were planted on graves in Mecca to signify the waiting time between the burial and the resurrection morning. Eastern poets spoke of the aloe as a symbol of bitterness and affliction, as did the Romans. The saying "As bitter as aloes" derives from the acrid taste of the medicines obtained from the plant. Aloe was one of the spices used to embalm the body of Christ.

AFTERTHOUGHT

MICHAELMAS DAISY — *Aster tradescanti*

"The Michaelmas Daisies, among dede weedes,
Blooms for St Michael's valourous deedes,
And seems the last of floures that stode,
Till the feste of St Simon and St Jude."
AN EARLY CALENDAR OF ENGLISH FLOWERS

A native of North America, the michaelmas daisy was introduced into English gardens in 1637 by Sir John Tradescant, son of John Tradescant the elder, who was gardener to Charles I. Also known as blue daisy, attic star, blue chamomile and starwort, it grows wild and is often seen on sea cliffs. It represents afterthought because it flowers so late — on or around St Michael's Day, 29 September (or 11 October, according to the old calendar) — when the flowers of summer have faded, coming unaware, like a surprising, pleasant thought. For the same reason, it often symbolizes "cheerfuless in old age".

AMIABILITY
and GOODNESS

<small>WHITE JASMINE</small> — *Jasminum officinale*

"And brides, as delicate and fair
As the white jasmine flowers they wear."
<small>THOMAS MOORE</small>

The sweet-scented jasmine, found along the ancient trade routes from Iran to China, was introduced to Britain in 1548. It came to represent amiability because its fragrance is so pleasing. There is a charming tale concerning a double-flowered variety, which the Grand Duke of Tuscany first procured in 1699. So determined was he to be the sole possessor of the plant that he strictly forbade his gardener to part with a single cutting. However, the gardener was in love, and so, on the birthday of his betrothed, he presented her with a nosegay, in the midst of which was a sprig of this rare jasmine. Charmed with its fragrance, the girl planted the sprig, which flourished. She then sold cuttings at a high price, earning enough to wed the gardener.

ANTICIPATION

<small>GOOSEBERRY</small> — *Ribes grossularia*

The gooseberry was popular in Tudor times. Thomas Tusser, who lived during the reign of Henry VIII, wrote:

"The Barberry, Respis and Gooseberry, too,
Look now to be planted as other things do."

It was grown in the famous kitchen garden at Nonesuch Palace at Ewell in Surrey. Later it became popular with the poor and, in 1740, gooseberry clubs were started. Here some enormous fruits were exhibited, some the size of ping-pong balls and weighing as much as two ounces each. To dream of ripe gooseberries is said to herald fortune, great fidelity in your sweetheart, many children (chiefly sons) and the accomplishment of your aims. Also called feaberry, dewberry and wineberry, its meaning, perhaps, has to do with anticipating the birth of a child, for they were always said to be found under gooseberry bushes.

ARDOUR

A R U M   L I L Y — *Arum maculatum*

"The lords and ladies dressed for masquerade
In green silk domino discreetly hooded."
VITA SACKVILLE WEST

One of the oldest of British wild flowers, the arum lily is a common sight in shady hedgerows in May. It is known by a variety of quaint country names: cuckoo pint or pintle, friar's cowl, priest's pintle or pilly, lords-and-ladies, Jack-in-the-pulpit, cows-and-bulls, ramp, starchwort and bloody men's fingers. Most refer to the obvious imagery inspired by the erect spadix, which begins to heat up around midday and give off a scent that attracts a variety of small flies, which then pollinate the flower. Implied is the erect pintle of the lustful cuckoo (the flower blossoms at the time the bird arrives) coming to father birds who ought not to be in the nest. Furthermore, the parson traditionally was the village 'cuckoo'. The flower's strange sexual symbolism was taken very seriously by superstitious farmers, who assessed the fertility of the forthcoming year's crop by the size of the arum's spadix – the bigger the better. The plant is sometimes known as Gethsemane and was supposed to have been sprinkled with the blood of Christ as it grew at the foot of the cross. Its erect structure led to it being claimed an aphrodisiac by Dioscorides, who added, "It is uretical too, and stirs up affections in conjunction with being drank with wine." Although the berries are highly poisonous and every part of the plant is acrid, the root contains a farinaceous substance, which, when properly prepared, and its acrid juice expressed, is good to eat – it is sold under the name of Portland Sago. Starch, too, has been made from the root and was used to stiffen Elizabethan ruffs and frills. Gerard, at the time of Elizabeth I, wrote "The most pure and white starch is made of the rootes of Cuckoo Pint; but most hurtfull for the hands of the laundresse that hath the handling of it, for it choppeth, blistereth, and maketh the hands rough and rugged, and withall smarting."

"How sweet it us'd to be, when April first
Unclos'd the arums leaves, and into view
Its ear-like spindling flowers their cases burst,
Beting'd with yellowish-white or lushy hue."
JOHN CLARE

ARGUMENT
FIG – *Ficus*

The fig is supposed to have been the first fruit tasted by man. A fig tree grew in Eden and, after Adam had eaten the forbidden apple, he tried to hide his nakedness with a fig leaf. The fig was dedicated to Juno and to Mercury and held sacred by the Romans because the tree's roots caught the cradle containing the infants Romulus and Remus as it was being swept along the Tiber. The meaning originates from an old quarrel between two soothsayers, Calchas and Mopsus, who challenged each other to guess the number of figs on a tree. Calchas failed the test and was so mortified he pined away and died. For the Jews, the fig is an emblem of peace and plenty, but in Italy it is looked on as a tree of ill omen because it is believed to be the tree on which Judas hanged himself. In India the fig, or banyan, tree is highly esteemed; one of the most venerated trees on earth. To dream of figs implies wealth, prosperity, happiness, the realisation of wishes and a contented old age.

ART, THE FINE ARTS

ACANTHUS – *Acanthus*

"Two bowls by the same skilful hand I've turn'd,
The handles round, and with green leaves adorn'd,
Of soft acanthus."

VIRGIL

The acanthus was a favourite plant amongst both the Greeks and Romans, who employed it for decorative purposes. Its leaves form the principal adornment of the Corinthian capital, modelled by Callimachus. The idea came to him when he was passing the grave of a young girl. At the base of the grave, over an acanthus root, her nurse had placed her bridal veil and other trinkets in a basket covered with a tile for protection. When the plant burst forth in spring around the basket, its progress was checked by the tile and the leaves were bent back. Callimachus was charmed by the accidental arrangement and incorporated it in the design of his column.

ARTIFICE
CLEMATIS — *Clematis flammula*

"The creeper, mellowing for an autumn blush;
And Virgin's Bower, trailing airily."
JOHN KEATS

The clematis is a great favourite in English gardens because of its mass of flowers and delicious fragrance. It can be trained over trellis to form shady arbours and is also known as virgin's bower, supposedly as a compliment, originally, to Elizabeth I. The juices are very acrid and can inflame the skin. Miller says of it that "If one leaf be cropped in a hot day in the summer season, and bruised, and presently put to the nostrils, it will cause a smell and pain like a flame." It represents artifice because beggars and gypsies, during the reign of Elizabeth I, used to press it to their flesh to make false ulcers – and some real sores – to try to excite compassion and charity.

"Clematis, wreath afresh thy garden bower."

AN ASSIGNATION
PIMPERNEL — *Anagallis arvensis*

Also known as John-go-to-bed-at-noon, poor man's weatherglass and shepherd's barometer, the pimpernel is the emblem of assignation because you can both tell the time and predict the weather by it. It invariably closes its petals before and during rain and opens them punctually at 7 am on fine days, closing them again at 2 pm. Old herbalists knew it as a surgical plant, capable of easing out arrows, thorns or splinters embedded in the flesh. The bruised leaves were believed to cure people who had been bitten by mad dogs and the juices were used for eye complaints. The best-selling author, Baroness Orczy, gave her aristocratic hero, Percy Blakeney, the codename The Scarlet Pimpernel in reference, no doubt, to the many secret assignations he had to make in order to save members of the French aristocracy from the guillotine during the French Revolution.

"No ear hath heard, no tongue can tell,
The virtues of the Pimpernell."

AUSTERITY

CARLINE OR COMMON THISTLE — *Carlina vulgaris*

"Cut your thistles before St John,
Or you'll have two instead of one."

"Thorns and Thistles shall it bring forth to thee" (Genesis IV). Thistles were part of the curse sent by God when man was made a tiller of the soil. The thistle has a contradictory nature. The symbol of austerity and rejection to some, it was regarded as a protective plant by others, sacred to the Virgin Mary, and to Thor to ward off thunder and lightning. It is also known as Our Lady's thistle and blessed thistle because the milk of the Virgin Mary was supposed to have fallen on it, giving it its distinctive milky appearance. The common thistle was named after Charles II because it was taken by him as an antidote to the plague. Once thought to have magical powers, the plant has a very ancient reputation in medicine and was deemed extremely useful in purifying the blood and assisting circulation. Dioscorides recommended the root to expel melancholy.

AVERSION

CHINA OR INDIAN PINK — *Dianthus Chinensis*

"With hues on hues expression cannot paint,
The breath of nature and her endless bloom."
JAMES THOMSON

The seeds of this species of Dianthus were first sent from China to Paris by French missionaries in 1705. In their single and double-flowering forms they became very popular in Victorian gardens. The Victorian writer Henry Phillips decided they should represent aversion "in allusion to the custom of the Chinese, who wish to avoid intercourse with other nations". In medieval art the pink was usually the symbol of divine love and signified that a lady was engaged to be married. They feature in paintings by Memling, Van Eyck and Rembrandt. Interestingly, the pink was not named after the colour — in fact the colour was named after the flower! The word 'pink', referring to colour, was first used in a description in 1720 and before that the colour we call pink was always described as flesh-coloured, blush or carnation.

BEAUTY
Rose – *Rosa*

*"Unkempt about those hedges blows
An English unofficial rose."*
Rupert Brooke

The rose has long been identified with female beauty. When Aphrodite, goddess of love, rose from the sea, the foam which covered her nakedness was said to have turned into white rose bushes as it fell to the ground. It was Aphrodite, too, who was said to have created the red rose. Running to comfort her fallen lover, Adonis, who had been gored by a wild boar, she scratched herself on the thorns of a rose bush and her blood turned its white blooms red. In Persian legend, a selfless nightingale impales itself on a white rosebush, turning the flowers red. The rose was thornless in paradise, according to another tradition: Eve plucked a bud as she was driven from the Garden of Eden and when Adam planted the slip, it came up surrounded by thorns as an everlasting reminder of their expulsion.

BEAUTY

Rose – *Rosa*

The rose's romantic associations were widely revived in the Middle Ages when the cult of the Virgin Mary was at its height. It is dedicated to her and the original rosary, devised by St Dominick, was in fact a string of beads made from tightly pressed rose petals which gave out a pleasing fragrance. The red rose is the rose of myth and legend, adopted by Christians as the symbol of the blood of martyrs. The white speaks of purity and silence and is often planted over the graves of the young and unmarried. It is thought unlucky if the petals fall as you pick a red or pink rose, but if the petals are shed from a white rose it means your angel is praying for you. The rose has been the emblem of England since 1461, when the warring Houses of Lancaster, identified by the red rose, and York, by the white, were reconciled by the marriage of Elizabeth of York and Henry of Lancaster and the two roses combined in the Tudor Rose. It remains prominent in English heraldry, signifying mercy and justice.

BENEFICENCE

POTATO — *Solanum tuberosum*

"Two large potatoes passed through a kitchen sieve
Unwonted softness to a salad give."

SIDNEY SMITH

A poor man's bread and a rich man's luxury, the potato richly deserves the epithet beneficence. A relative newcomer to Europe, the plant was introduced from North America by Sir Walter Raleigh's colonists in 1586. John Gerard called it "the potato of Virginia" or "bastard potatoes", to distinguish it from the sweet potato so highly prized by the Elizabethans and includes it in the list of plants he was growing in his garden in Holborn in 1596. The potato was ascribed remarkable, almost magical, curative properties. William Salmon declared it to be: "moderately Diuretick, Stomatick, Chylisick, Analeptick and Spermatogenick. They nourish the whole body, restore consumption, and provoke Lust." It rapidly became the main source of vitamins for the peasant class and was said to cure rheumatism, frostbite, chilblains, toothache and warts.

BIRTH

DITTANY — *Origanum dictamnus*

The Dittany of Crete was consecrated to the goddess Lucina, who presided over the birth of children and she was often represented wearing a crown of dittany. Greek and Roman women believed the plant had extraordinary properties which facilitated childbirth. The root was particularly recommended by the oracle of Phthas and, according to Virgil, Venus used the plant to heal the wounded Æneas. Indeed, it had a high reputation as a wound-herb. Theophrastus reports that it was eaten by goats in Crete to expel arrows that had struck them; Gerard confirms this and adds that it was most useful in drawing forth splinters of wood and bones and healing wounds, "especially those made with invenomed weapons, arrowes, shot out of guns, or such like". The juice, he says, is so powerful that by its mere smell it "drives away venomous beasts, and doth astonish them". When mixed with wine, the juice was also considered a remedy for snake bites. Astrologers say that dittany is under the dominion of Mars.

BLUNTNESS

BORAGE — *Borago officinalis*

This meaning may derive from the appearance of the plant: its stalks and leaves are covered with a rough, hairy substance although the effect is softened by its bright blue flowers. In Arabia borage is known as 'father of sweat' and used to be given to produce sweat to take the edge off a fever. Its medicinal uses appear in almost every old herbal: John Evelyn said it revived the hypochondriac and cheered the hardworking student; Parkinson commended it for expelling "pensiveness and melancholy", and Culpeper prescribed it for putrid and pestilential fever, jaundice and rheumatism. Its cooling and soothing properties have traditionally been employed in drinks as well as medicine: the Greeks and Romans put sprays of borage into wine cups to cool the wine — just as we do now with Pimms — and Gerard said, "The leaves and floures of Borage put into wine make men and women glad and merry and drive away all sadness, dullness and melancholy." Wet nurses drank herb soups that contained borage in the belief that it would encourage their milk.

BLUSHES

MARJORAM — *Origanum*

"Bind your brows with the flowers of sweet smelling marjoram."
CATULLUS

Marjoram is a tender plant and the scaly leaves in some species are tinged a delicate red as though blushing. The Greeks and Romans called it the herb of happiness and used it to crown their young lovers. It has a very appealing, sweet scent — according to Greek myth, marjoram was originally the name of a serving boy in the court of King Cinyras of Cyprus, who, when he dropped and broke a jar of rare perfume, collapsed in terror and was transformed into the sweet-smelling herb. Marjoram was highly thought of in the physic garden, and the Elizabethans used it with sage and rosemary boiled in wine to treat black teeth. Parkinson said it was much in demand by ladies "to put in nosegays" and to use "in sweet powders, sweet bags and sweet washing waters".

45

BONDS OF LOVE
HONEYSUCKLE – *Lonicera*

"I will wind thee in my arms.
So doth the woodbine, the sweet honeysuckle,
Gently entwist."

WILLIAM SHAKESPEARE

Samuel Pepys called it the "trumpet flower" and wrote, "The ivory bugles blow scent instead of sound." Honeysuckle has a variety of local names: lamps of scent, suckles, gramophone horns, bugle bands, evening pride, bindweed, and its oldest name, woodbine. William Bullein wrote in his *Book of Simples* in 1562: "How friendly doth this herbe, if I may name it, imbrace the bodies, arms and braunches of trees, wyth his long winding stalkes and tender leaves, opening or spreading forth his sweete lilies, like ladies' fingers, among the thornes." Honeysuckle has always been known as the emblem of captive love because of the marks it makes on other plants as it twines about them.

CALUMNY

HELLEBORE — *Helleborus niger*

Hellebores have a romantic history and for centuries were thought to cure madness and counteract witchcraft. Pieces of root were inserted in a hole cut through the ear or dewlap of a sick animal with the idea of warding off evil spirits. On the root's removal twenty-four hours later, the trouble was supposed to be cured. It is certainly a highly poisonous plant, with various medicinal properties including that of heart stimulant. In ancient times, anyone collecting the plant took stringent precautions, first eating garlic, then circling the plant with a sword and turning to the East to offer a prayer to Apollo for leave to dig up the root. And all the while they looked out for eagles, for should one approach, the gatherer would die within the year. The ancient Gauls are said to have rubbed the points of their arrows with hellebore, believing that it made game more tender. Known as Christmas rose, winter rose or flower of St Agnes, it is still planted near cottage doors – a link with the past, when it was planted to prevent evil spirits entering.

CELIBACY
ROSEBAY WILLOW HERB — *Epilobium angustifolium*

The French call this plant *Laurier Saint Antoine*, after St Anthony, the founder of monasteries, which has led to it becoming known as the flower of celibacy. Its fruity and rather sickly scent has encouraged a host of country names: codlings-and-cream, goosebery pie, gooseberry plant, cherry pie and apple pie. It is also known as blooming-Sally, fireweed and, in parts of Scotland, king's sceptre or king's rod, fairy wand and bloody fingers. Gerard describes the rosebay variety as a "goodly and statelie plant having leaves like the great willow or ozier and garnished with brave flowers of great beautie". It is rarely seen in formal gardens because the slightest breeze wafts the silky seeds away, which then grow rapidly wherever they fall, particularly on land cleared by burning — hence the name fireweed. During and after the Second World War, the bombsites of London became pink with the rose spikes of willow herb. The leaves of the rosebay willow herb have been used as a substitute for tea, especially popular in Russia.

CHARITY
TURNIP — *Rapa*

Turnips were highly regarded by Romans of all classes, not merely as delicious vegetables, but also as an aid to good health. Columella urged that turnips be grown in abundance, arguing that any surplus could be fed to animals, and Pliny considered them second only to corn in both financial and practical worth. He tells of roots weighing as much as forty pounds. Turnips featured on heraldic shields to indicate the person was of good disposition and relieved the poor. They were a sixteenth-century cure for hoarseness, coughs and gout and the juice was used to temper steel for knives, daggers and swords. According to the herbalists, turnips were an aphrodisiac, and could also be used as a beauty preparation and to improve the sight. A favourite Elizabethan dish was turnips stuffed with minced meat. However, in Westphalia, if turnips were set before a young man by the lady he was courting, they signified that he was totally unacceptable to her and, in Plymouth, to say "She has given him turnips" means she has cold-shouldered him. To dream of turnips denotes fruitless toil.

CHASTITY

ORANGE BLOSSOM — *Citrus aurantium*

"These rapid fly, more heard than seen
Mid orange-boughs of polished green,
With glowing fruit, and flowers between of purest white."

Pure white orange blossom is firmly associated with brides, who wear it wreathed in garlands on their brows as a symbol of maiden purity and chastity. The custom, in fact, originated with the Saracens, for whom the orange-flower was a sign of a happy, prosperous and fecund marriage. In Crete, the bride and bridegroom are sprinkled with orange-flower water, and in Sardinia it is customary to attach oranges to the horns of the oxen which draw the bridal carriage. One of the rare attractions of the orange is that fruit, blossom and leaves are on the tree at the same time. The scented blossom has narcotic properties which induce sleep when taken as a tisane. An orange symbolizes generosity in the language of flowers.

CHEERFULNESS
in ADVERSITY

CHINESE CHRYSANTHEMUM — *Chrysanthemum Indicum*

"In the second month the Peach-tree blooms,
But not till the ninth the Chrysanthemums:
So each must wait till his own time comes."

OLD CHINESE PROVERB

Long-held in high esteem in the Orient, chrysanthemums were grown by the Chinese as early as 500 BC. The Mikado adopted them as his personal emblem in AD 797 and for a time their cultivation was restricted to the gardens of the emperor and nobility. The Japanese held chrysanthemum exhibitions in AD 900, using them to construct models of their gods or heroes. The 'rising sun' in the Japanese flag represents not the sun but a chrysanthemum, with a central disc and sixteen flaring petals. They were introduced to England in 1764 by Miller and cultivated at Chelsea Physic Garden. They signify cheerfulness in adversity because their glorious blooms brighten November.

CHILDISHNESS

BUTTERCUPS AND KINGCUPS – *Ranunculus bulbosus*

"Oh! I can now recall th'unthrift delight
That filled my basket and my tiny hand,
With Buttercups that shone in burnished gold"
MISS TWAMLEY

To Shakespeare the buttercup was cuckoo-bud; it is also known as goldcup and giltcup, gold-knob and leopard's foot. Children adore them and they feature in many of their games and rhymes. "Do you like butter?" they say, holding a buttercup under another child's chin to see if a gold reflection is a brilliant affirmation. Once it was believed that if the root of a buttercup was hung in a linen cloth round the neck of a lunatic "in the waine of the moon when the signe was in the first degree of Taurus or Scorpio", he would be cured. Ben Jonson wrote:

"Fair ox-ey, goldylocks and columbine,
Pinks, gentian, King-cups and sweet sops-in-wine."

50

CHIVALRY

DAFFODIL — *Narcissus pseudonarcissus*

"I wandered lonely as a cloud
That floats on high o'er vales and hills,
When all at once I saw a crowd,
A host of golden daffodils;
Beside the lake, beneath the trees,
Fluttering and dancing in the breeze.

Continuous as the stars that shine
And twinkle on the milky way,
They stretched in never-ending line . . ."
WILLIAM WORDSWORTH

Gerard knew this yellow flower as daffodowndilly, but it was also called daff-lilies, affodyle, chalice flower, lent-lily and lent-cock. Proserpine was gathering them when she was seized and carried off to the underworld by Pluto.

CLEANLINESS
HYSSOP — *Hyssopus officinalis*

"Purge me with hyssop and I shall be clean."
PSALM 51

In ancient times hyssop, originally called *azob*, was a holy herb used by the Hebrews to cleanse sacred places; in the Middle Ages it was strewn in palaces, banqueting halls and grand houses. It keeps its scent when dried and is used in potpourris or, distilled into oil, in perfumes. John Ray, in his *British Flora* of 1670, relates how a man who was violently kicked on the thigh by a horse was poulticed with boiled hyssop. The pain instantly ceased and within a few hours no bruises could be seen. The Romans used it as a digestive and it is also credited with curing toothache, head lice, rheumatism and anaemia. Gerard believed "a decoction of Hyssope made with figges, water, honey and rue, and drunken, helpeth the old cough". To dream of hyssop portends that friends will be instrumental to your peace and happiness.

COLD-HEARTEDNESS
LETTUCE — *Lactuca*

The ancient Egyptians grew lettuce, as did the Greeks and the Romans, who served them as an hors d'oeuvre after blanching them under a flat stone. Pliny stated that lettuces of all descriptions were thought to cause sleep and Pope, referring to these soporific qualities, said:

"If your wish be rest,
Lettuce and Cowslip wine, probatum est."

Lettuce was valued as a sedative and as a treatment for headaches and indigestion. John Parkinson thought it an excellent bromide and impishly wrote: 'It abateth bodily lust and therefore both it and rue are commended for Monkes, Nunnes and the like of people to eat, and use to keep them chaste; it represeth also venerous dreams, and applyed to the Cods with a little Campfire [camphor], abateth the pride and heate of lust which some call the Coltes evill."

COMFORT
GERANIUM (SCARLET) – *Geranium*

Many species of geranium were introduced to England from South Africa in the eighteenth and nineteenth century, but what is called the English geranium, the crane's bill, dates from the sixteenth century. It is also known as stork's-bill, pelican's-bill and heron's-bill, in reference to the characteristically long and noticeable 'beak' of the carpel. While the wild geranium (G. *robertianum*) is in some places linked to Robin Hood and known as herb Robert and Robin's eyes. The seed vessel of the plant, noted for its sharp point, is known as pook-needle, or the needle employed by the fairies. Culpeper wrote that herb-Robert would stay blood, heal wounds and cure ulcers. The meaning of the flower changes with its colour: rose or pink signify preference; scarlet, comfort; nutmeg, an unexpected meeting; silver-leaved, recollection; dark, melancholy; ivy, bridal favour , and oak-leaved, true friendship. Wild geraniums signify steadfast piety. To dream of geraniums means "a change of interests."

CONCEALED MERIT
CORIANDER – *Coriandrum sativum*

According to the Chinese, coriander seeds had the power to bestow immortality. The Romans, who, according to Pliny, imported the best coriander seeds from Egypt, used the plant to flavour a variety of dishes, including flamingo and fungi. They also brought it to Britain, where records show it was cultivated in Saxon gardens, monasteries and, by the fifteenth century, had become an important pot-herb. The seeds were crystalized and served as a sweetmeat by the Elizabethans, which may explain the meaning. It has many medicinal uses, including the ability to expel flatulence – "concealed" as comfits, it was generally given to women and children for this purpose. The seeds are chiefly used to disguise the unpleasant taste of medicine – but if used too freely they become narcotic. It has long been used in the East, where the seeds became an ingredient of Indian curry powder. Its generic name derives from the Greek *koris*, 'bed-bug', on account of the appearance of the seeds and the pungent odour of the leaves, which has been compared to the smell of ticks.

CONFIDENCE
Polyanthus – *Polyanthus*

The polyanthus is made emblem of confidence because the plants are exceptionally vigorous, come in many colours and "when in bloom release so powerful a perfume from an acre field that it may be noticed from a distance of a mile". The flower was probably created by crossing coloured primroses with cowslips and was first mentioned in 1665 by John Rea, a nurseryman and author of *Flora, Ceres and Pomona*. He called it the red cowslip or big oxlip, "bearing many flowers on one stalk, in fashion like those of the field but of several red colours". Rea's daughter, Miranda, married the Revd Samuel Gilbert, who refers to the flower in his *Florist's Vade Mecum*: 'There are several oxlips or polyanthuses; I have very large hose-in-hose of deeper or lighter reds." The first illustration, of a crimson-purple flower, appeared in John Hill's famous, twenty-five volume work *The Vegetable Kingdom* in 1759. In the eighteenth century, double polyanthuses were known as pug-in-a-pinner.

CONSOLATION

Snowdrop — *Galanthus nivalis*

"The Snowdrop, in purest white arraie,
First rears her hedde on Candlemas daie."
An Early Calendar of English Flowers

Also known as fair maids of February, candlemas bells, Mary's tap-
ers and bulbous violet, snowdrops are aptly made the emblem of
consolation and hope since they are the first flowers to appear after
winter, cheering us with the promise of spring. They were supposedly
sacred to virgins and are often found growing in the orchards attached
to convents and old monastic buildings. They are also dedicated to the
Virgin Mary and were strewn before her image as signs of purity and
chastity. They are said to have sprung up in a ring where an angel stood
consoling Eve over the barrenness of the Garden of Eden in winter.
Fable has it that the angel caught a falling flake of snow, breathed on it
and bade it take form, and flourish.

CONSTANCY

"There thou shalt cull me simples, and shall teach
Thy friend the name and healing pow'rs of each,
From the tall blue-bell to the dwarfish weed,
What the dry land, and what the marshes breed."
JOHN MILTON

Common in woodlands, fields and hedgerows, the bluebell is an enchanting flower. Robert Burns named it "constancy with its unchanging blue". Gerard knew it as the English jacinth or blue harebell and describes the flowers as having "a strong sweet smell, somewhat stuffing the head". He also called it "Steeple Milkie Bell-Flower", because of the milky nature of the juices secreted by the flower stalks. The Elizabethans used this sticky substance as a starch for linen and to bind their books. Gerard reports that it was also used for setting feathers upon arrows. In the eighteenth century it was used medicinally as a diuretic. A century later Tennyson speaks of bluebell juice being used to cure snake bite.

COQUETRY

"The light coquettes in sylphs aloft repair,
And sport and flutter in the fields of air."
ALEXANDER POPE

The yellow day lily signifies coquetry because its fragile flower seldom lasts a second day. However, although the blossoms are not long-lasting, they are succeeded by others daily through the month of June, so that the plant continues to display its beauty. In France it is called *belle d'un jour*. They have flourished in English gardens for centuries and Gerard, writing in 1596, records, "These Lillies do growe in my garden, and also in the gardens of herbarists and louers of fine and rare plants." The dried flowers are used by the Chinese in soups, various meat dishes and with noodles and sold under such names as gum-jum or gum-tsoy. They are somewhat gelatinous and, when chewed, are supposed to cure toothache.

COURAGE

BLACK POPLAR – *Populus nigra*

"A double wreath Evander twined,
And poplars black and white his temple bind."
VIRGIL

Pitying the intense grief of the Heliades, sisters of the rash Phaethon (who had yoked his horses to the chariot of the Sun and thus perished), the gods turned them into black poplars and their tears to amber. The poplar was consecrated to the goddess Proserpine and the demi-god Hercules, who sometimes wore a crown of poplar leaves – hence its meaning. In France the poplar is regarded as a Republican emblem and, during the Revolution of 1848, poplars were transplanted from gardens and set up in the squares of Paris, where they were glorified as trees of Liberty and hung with wreaths of everlasting flowers. Napoleon III had them all uprooted and burnt. The white poplar symbolizes time in the language of flowers because its leaves are dark on one side and light on the other, emblematic of night and day.

CRIMINALITY

TAMARISK – *Tamarix*

"On yon rough craig,
Where the wild tamarisk whistles to the sea blast."
HUMPHREY DAVY

The tamarisk is a special tree for the Egyptians as it was said to have shielded the dead body of Osiris from Typhon. In Persia the Magian priests used a thin bundle of tamarisk twigs, called a *baresma*, to divine future events. The Romans used it to garland criminals. According to tradition, it was from tamarisk trees that the showers of manna descended on the famished Israelites in the desert and to this day, Bedouin Arabs collect and make into cakes a sweet, mucilaginous sugar which seeps from the stems of T. *gallica* and T. *mannifera*. It was believed to have magical powers and Pliny recommended it for "night-foes", although adding that the tree was "unluckie" since it never bore fruit and was accursed, used, as it was, to garland criminals.

CRUELTY
S<small>TINGING</small> N<small>ETTLE</small> – *Urtica urens*

"Nettles with tender shoots to cleanse the blood."
S<small>TREET</small> H<small>AWKER'S</small> C<small>RY</small>

The stinging nettle's reputation for cruelty is due, of course, to its protective feature – the stinging hairs on the leaves and stem which release formic acid when touched. Although largely ignored and even disliked nowadays, in the past it had many uses. It was an ancient textile plant and cloth from its fibres was being woven in Scotland as late as the eighteenth century. Nettle oil preceded paraffin, and the juice, which curdles milk, was once used instead of rennet to make cheese. Nettle tea, rich in vitamin C, was meant to be a good cure for colds and a beneficial gargle. Worn on the person in times of danger, nettles were believed to drive out fear and inspire courage; they were also held to be a protection against evil spirits. To dream of being stung means disappointment; but to dream of gathering nettles augurs well.

DANGER

R H O D O D E N D R O N – *Rhododendron*

"O'er pine-clad hills, and dusky plains,
In silent state rhododendron reigns,
And spreads, in beauty's softest blooms,
Her purple glories through the glooms."
                                                    GEORGE SHAW

The danger signified by the rhododendron lurks in its flowers, for honey made from their pollen can be poisonous. Frank Kingdon Ward, during a plant-hunting trip in the Himalayas, came upon a wild bees' nest in rhododendron country. His bearers, tired of their monotonous diet, gorged themselves on the fresh honey and, as a result, became so intoxicated as to be practically unconscious for days. However, this toxic property disappears as the honey ages; it can also be dispersed by heating. The *Rhododendron crysanthum* is native to Siberia, where it was used as a remedy for rheumatism and gout.

DAUNTLESSNESS
Thrift — *Statice armeria*

"From the border lines,
Composed of daisy and resplendent thrift,
Flowers straggling forth had on those paths encroached,
Which they were used to deck."

WILLIAM WORDSWORTH

Thrift thrives in wild, desolate places. Growing high up on cliff faces and steep hillsides, resisting storms and cutting blasts, it was thus made emblem of dauntlessness. In the time of Elizabeth I, it was called ladies' cushion, pincushion or sea-gilloflower. Other common names include sea-pink, swift, French-pink, sea-grass and salt-rose. Gerard says that "the use of the plant in physicke is not yet knowen, neither doth any seek into the nature thereof, but esteeme him onely for beautie and pleasure in gardens". It is often used as a border plant in both formal and cottage gardens.

DEATH
and ETERNAL SORROW
Cypress — *Cupressus*

The cypress is an ancient and sacred tree, surrounded by many myths and legends. The Persians believed it had its origins in paradise; in Cyprus (which derived its name from the tree) a goddess, Beroth, personified by the tree, was worshipped. Christ's cross, Cupid's dart, Moses' rod, Hercules' club and Noah's Ark are all said to have been made from cypress wood and certainly it was employed in ancient time in ship-building. Yet, despite these associations, in all countries from the earliest time it has been the emblem of woe and sorrow. Horace, Virgil and Ovid all refer to it as a tree both gloomy and funereal, and its shadow was thought to be unfortunate. The Greeks and Romans consecrated the 'sad' tree to Pluto and Proserpine, as well as to the Fates and Furies. Cypresses were planted around graves, for they were esteemed as undying trees, ever verdant and fragrant and, as such, a sign of eternal life. To dream of a cypress tree denotes affliction or obstruction in business.

DECEITFUL CHARMS
or DECEIT
THORN APPLE – *Datura stramonium*

The thorn apple has a bad reputation. In France it is called *herbe du diable* and *pomme du diable*. The whole plant has a foetid, disagreeable smell when bruised and, carelessly used, can be very poisonous. Despite this it does have various medicinal uses: in the treatment of asthma and bronchial complaints, for instance; and Gerard guarantees that, when boiled with hog's grease and made into a salve, it will cure inflammations, burnings and scaldings "as well of fire, water, boiling lead, gunpowder, as that which comes by lightning". High doses can be dangerous and in India – where it grows abundantly – thieves, assassins and prostitutes administer it to their victims to make them insensible. Stramonium (from *Datura*) is a common source of 'knock-out' drops and produces strange dreams. In India thorn apple is known as the drunkard, the madman, the deceiver and the fool-maker. It is also called the tuft of Siva, Siva being the god of destruction.

DECEPTION
WINTER CHERRY – *Physalis alkekengi*

The winter cherry is a graceful little shrub with white flowers and, later, scarlet berries about the size of cherries. It signifies deception because, although the berries assume the beauty of cherries in shape, gloss and colouring, they are not what they seem. The winter cherry was common in Gerard's time, as he observes, "The Redde Winter Cherrie growth vpon olde broken wals about the borders of fieldes, and in moist shadowie places, and in most gardens, where some conserue it for the beautie of the berries, and others for the great and worthy vertues thereof."

"Sigh no more, ladies, sigh no more;
Men were deceivers ever:
One foot in the sea, and one on shore;
To one thing constant never."
WILLIAM SHAKESPEARE

61

DELICACY

CORNFLOWER — *Centaurea cyanus*

"There is a flower, a purple flower,
Sown by the wind, nursed by the shower,
O'er which Love breathed a powerful spell,
The truth of whispering hope to tell.
Now, gentle flower, I pray thee tell,
If my love loves me, and loves me well,
So May the fall of the morning's dew
Keep the sun from fading they tender blue."

In classical legend Flora, the goddess of flowers, was worshipped by the youth Cyanus. On finding him dead in a cornfield one day, Flora transformed him into the cornflower in honour of his devoted love and sensitivity, which is why the flower has become the emblem of delicacy. From earliest times painters pounded the petals of the cornflower to make a delicate ultramarine paste.

DESPAIR

MARIGOLD — *Calendula officinalis*

*"As emblem of my heart's sad grief,
Of flow'rs, the marigold is chief."*

The marigold has a mournful reputation, associated as it is with grief, pain and chagrin. However, such sorrowful sentiments may be tempered by mixing the flower with others. Combine it with roses, for example, and the message becomes 'the sweet sorrows of love'; alone, it expresses ennui and despair; woven with a variety of flowers it represents the ever-varying course of life, a mixture of good and bad; a bouquet of marigolds and poppies says, "I will soothe your grief." Dedicated to the Virgin Mary and known as Mary's gold, it was held in high esteem by herbalists, who recommended it "to comfort heart and spirits". The most moving reference to it as a symbol of despair was made by Charles I when prisoner in Carisbrooke Castle: "The Marigold observes the sun/More than my Subjects me have done . . . "

DIFFIDENCE

Cyclamen – *Cyclamen*

Cyclamen has many local names, including sow-bread, swine-bread, ivy-leaved cyclamen and bleeding nun. The Romans called it *Tuber terræ* on account of its turnip-like root. The fresh tubers can be made into an ointment and applied externally as a liniment or poultice. In the seventeenth century it was used to prevent pitting after smallpox and as a complexion wash, especially after yellow jaundice. The tubers were fed to pigs, hence the name sow-bread, but were also baked and made into cakes, eaten for their tonic and aphrodisiac properties. It was used by midwives, who, regarding the root with superstitious reverence, would wear it while tending to women in their confinement. Gerard was so convinced of the plant's ability to assist birth that he fenced the cyclamens in his garden with sticks, and laid others crossways over them, in case a pregnant woman should, merely by stepping over them, bring on a miscarriage. The plant's meaning is suggested by the fact that, although the flower expands its petals, it never rears its head to the sun.

DIGNITY

Magnolia – *Magnolia grandiflora*

"He told of the magnolia spread
High as a cloud, high overhead."
William Wordsworth

Magnolias take their name from Pierre Magnol (1638-1715), Professor of Botany and Medicine at Montpellier, where he established the Botanic Garden. "It is handsome both in foliage and flower and worthy of so fine a man," wrote Linnaeus. In the United States, the magnificent blossoms of the magnolia and their shiny green leaves advance above the forest trees, displaying their dignity and dispensing their fragrance. It has been adopted as the state flower of Louisiana and Mississippi. The bark, if chewed, is said to cure tobacco addiction and the plant has been used for centuries as a medicine for rheumatism, fevers, catarrh, malaria and gout. An infusion of the bark is said to arrest the paroxysms in fever and have a stimulating and tonic effect.

DISDAIN

YELLOW CARNATION — *Dianthus*

"The fairest flowers o' the season
Are our Carnations, and streak'd Gillyflowers,
Which some call, nature's bastards: of that kind
Our rustic garden's barren; and I care not
To get slips of them."

WILLIAM SHAKESPEARE

Carnations were said to grow in Paradise. In Elizabethan times brides were given wine flavoured with carnations to drink after the wedding ceremony. Their meaning in the language of flowers changes depending on their colour: a striped carnation signals refusal; a yellow one disdain; while red pleads eloquently, "Alas for my poor heart." Ancient tradition suggests the flower sprang from the graves of young lovers. In his *Love Letters Made of Flowers*, Leigh Hunt spoke of expressing:

"One's sighs and passionate declarations
In odorous rhetoric of carnations."

DISTINCTION

CARDINAL FLOWER — *Lobelia cardinalis*

"In the wind and tempest of fortune's frown,
Distinction, with a broad and powerful fan,
Puffing at all, winnows the light away."

WILLIAM SHAKESPEARE

Lobelia cardinalis was apparently introduced to England in 1629 from Canada (then a French colony) by John Tradescant, gardener to Charles I, who sent it to Henrietta Maria, Charles I's Queen. She, it is said, laughed excessively on seeing the flowers and said their colour reminded her of the scarlet stockings of a cardinal. (Its shape is not altogether dissimilar to a cardinal's hat, either.) John Parkinson therefore called it the cardinal flower in his *Paradisi in sole Paradisus Terrestris* (1629) which he later published and dedicated to Her Majesty. It earned its meaning by the vivid hue of its flower, which the French author Alphonse Karr said would make even the verbena pale before it.

DRUNKENNESS

Vine — *Vitus vinifera*

"Great father, Bacchus, to my song repair;
For clust'ring grapes are thy peculiar care."

The grape vine is sacred to Bacchus, that jovial, gregarious god, who is invariably depicted wearing a crown of vine-leaves and carrying a bunch of grapes. There are many references to the vine and vine culture in the Bible: Noah planted a vineyard, and in Leviticus there is a command that, every seventh year, the vines were to be left untouched by the pruning knife. Anacharsis said that the vine bore three kinds of fruit: intoxication, voluptuousness and repentance. Culpeper states that the vine is "a gallant tree of the Sun, very sympathetical with the body of man; and that is the reason spirits of wine is the greatest cordial among all vegetables". Walter Scott wrote fondly:

"Let dimpled mirth his temples twine,
With tendrils of the laughing Vine."

EARLY YOUTH

PRIMROSE — *Primula vulgaris*

The primrose, a Celtic fairy flower, represents the age between childhood and womanhood and thus symbolizes purity and youth. Its early blossom and delicate perfume are cheering heralds to summer. Shakespeare observed the early appearance of the flowers when few insects are around and, in *The Winter's Tale*, commented on the "pale primroses that die unmarried". The name derives from the medieval Latin *prima rosa*, the first or earliest flower of the year. The common primrose (yellow) is dedicated to St Agatha; the red variety to St Adelaide, and the early red to St Theodora. The first posy brought into the house had to contain at least thirteen flowers, otherwise the hens would lay badly.

> "Primrose, first-born child of Ver,
> Merry springtime's harbinger,
> With her bells dim."
> WILLIAM SHAKESPEARE

EGOTISM
NARCISSUS — *Narcissus*

"Narcissus on the grassy verdure lies;
But whilst within the crystal font he tries
To quench his heat, he feels new heats arise,
For as his own bright image he survey'd
He fell in love with the fantastic shade."

Narcissus was a beautiful young man of whom it had been foretold he should live happily until he beheld his own face. Passionately loved by the unhappy Echo and caressed by the Nymphs, he nevertheless slighted and rejected their advances. One day he stopped to quench his thirst in a stream and for the first time saw his own reflection. Instantly smitten with his own beauty, he was transfixed to the spot, where he pined away and died. According to Ovid, the flower known by his name sprang from his corpse and the cup at the centre of the flower is fabled to contain his tears. The flower is also known as London pride, eggs and butter, sweet nancies, pheasant's eye and poet's narcissus.

ELEGANCE
ACACIA (PINK) OR LOCUST TREE — *Robinia pseudoacacia*

"Along the rail fences the locust trees were in bloom. The breeze
caught their perfume and wafted it down the road. Every
Virginian remembers those locusts which grow along the
highways: their cloud-shaped masses of blue-green foliage and
heavy drooping clusters of cream-white flowers like pea blossoms."
                                                    WILLA CATHER

The robinia is one of the most beautiful of all trees, its wood is extremely hard and many of the first houses in Boston were built of it. Elegant in blossom, it scents the whole air. A sprig of acacia is specially revered by Freemasons, who make a practice of dropping twigs of the plant on the coffins of brethren. "The acacia, together with that from Virginia, deserves a place among our avenue trees," wrote John Evelyn in 1664. The yellow acacia symbolizes secret love.

ENCHANTMENT
Vervain — *Verbena officinalis*

"She night-shade strews to work him ill,
Therewith the Vervain, and her dill,
That hind'reth witches of their will."
Michael Drayton

Vervain is a very ancient symbol of enchantment, once used in divinations, sacrificial rites, potions and incantations. The Greeks called it the sacred herb and used it to cleanse the festival table of Jupiter before solemn occasions. It was as important as mistletoe to Druids, who only cut the plant when neither the sun nor moon was visible and afterwards poured honey and honeycomb on the earth as atonement for robbing it of so precious a herb. "The enchanter's plant", it was gathered by witches to do mischief, although it could also be used to combat them and was said by Drayton to be " 'gainst witchcraft much avayling". In the seventeenth century it was called Mercury's-moist-blood, Juno's tears, pigeon's grass, simpler's joy and herb of grace.

ENVY
Bramble — *Rubus fruticosus*

The bramble has many religious associations. The Crown of Thorns was said to be made of it and it was also supposed to have been the burning bush in which Jehovah appeared to Moses. In the Old Testament it was chosen to rule over the giants of the plant kingdom and it was believed that, as Satan was cast out of Paradise, he fell into a bramble bush, cursing it roundly. He is now said to spit (or less delicately, to urinate) on the plant on the anniversary of the Fall, hence the superstition that it is unwise to eat blackberries after Old St Michaelmas Day, 11 October, as they will be sour. Sick children were passed through a branch of bramble that had rooted at both ends in order to cure a variety of ills. To dream of passing through places covered with brambles usually portends troubles: if they prick you, secret enemies will do you injury; if they draw blood, expect heavy losses in trade; but, emerge unhurt and you will triumph.

ERROR

BEE ORCHID — *Ophrys apifera*

"See on that flowret's velvet breast,
How close the busy vagrant lies!
His thin-wrought plume, his downy breast,
The ambrosial gold that swells his thighs.

Perhaps his fragrant load may bind
His limbs; we'll set the captive free;
I sought the living bee to find,
And found the picture of a bee."

JOHN LANGHORN

This most beautiful orchid is the symbol of error because nature appears to have sprinkled the stem with bees instead of flowers. Their ordinary habitat is open meadows, by woodsides and in chalky soils. In the past the trompe l'oeil effect of the flower might easily have been overlooked in such rural places – not so now they are so rare.

FAITHFULNESS and MODESTY
Violet — *Viola odorata*

"Violet is for faithfulness,
Which in me shall abide:
Hoping likewise that from your heart
You will not let it slide."

The sweet-scented violet was an ancient flower of love chosen by the Greeks for its perfume as Aphrodite's flower. It was widely used during ancient times as a cure for headaches, melancholia and insomnia. Timorous or retiring girls are frequently called 'shrinking violets' and the plant has long been associated with modesty and faithfulness. It was Queen Victoria's favourite flower and also Napoleon Bonaparte's. While the latter was in exile in Elba, his supporters, forced underground, identified one another by the violets they wore as badges. Napoleon picked blooms from the grave of his beloved Josephine, which were later found in a locket on his death bed.

71

FALSEHOOD

Viper's Bugloss — *Echium vulgare* and *Anchusa*

B ugloss was perhaps the most ancient, as well as the most innocent, of all preparations for the face. A rouge capable of lasting
several days, which washing only refreshed, was made from its roots —
hence its reputation for falsehood. Some Native Americans used the
roots of the indigenous *Anchusa virginica* to paint their bodies red. It was
used by the Greeks and Romans to give an agreeable colour to their
ointments; they also used it to colour wood and wax, as well as to stain
wool. Viper's bugloss derives its name from its seeds, which resemble
the head of a viper, and also because, according to Matthiolus, Nican-
der and Dioscorides, it was a potent cure for snake bites. Parkinson
wrote "The water distilled in glasses or the roote itself taken is good
against the passions and tremblings of the heart as also against
swooning, sadness and melancholy."

FATE

Flax — *Linum*

"Courage uncertain dangers may abate;
But, who can bear the approach of certain fate?"
JOHN DRYDEN

F lax was the hieroglyphic of fate among the Egyptians, who also
cultivated it for its valuable fibres, which were then used in the
manufacture of linen and paper. It was one of the first textiles used by
man and Herodotus describes the Egyptian priests wearing linen gar-
ments made from its fibres, specimens of which can still be seen today
in museums, enfolding Egyptian mummies. There are many superstitions connected with sowing flax: it will only flower at the time of
day at which it was originally sown; stolen seeds mingled with the rest
cause the crop to thrive; it acts as a talisman against witchcraft and
sorcery, wounds and accidents.

"How sweetly blooms
Upon the slopes the azure-blossomed flax."
NOEL THOMAS CARRINGTON

FEAST
or BANQUET
PARSLEY — *Apium petroselinum*

"Let parsley spread
Its living verdure o'er the feast."
HORACE

Parsley occupied a noble place in ancient culture. The leaves were woven into garlands for heroes, both of war and the Grecian games, and were worn at marriage feasts. The seeds were used in aromatic salts by the Romans and the fresh leaves in sauces and gourmet dishes. Charlemagne was particularly fond of cheese flavoured with parsley seeds. In Elizabethan times, meatballs were cooked with parsley, and mutton boiled with the roots. Medicinally it was used for liver and kidney complaints and mixed with breadcrumbs or flour to make poultices. Culpeper valued parsley:

"It is very comfortable to the stomach . . . good for wind and to remove obstructions both of the liver and spleen . . . Galen commendeth it for the falling sickness . . . the seed is effectual to break the stone and ease the pain and torments thereof . . . The leaves of parsley laid to the eyes that are inflamed with heat or swollen, relieves them if it be used with bread or meat . . . The juice dropped into the ears with a little wine easeth the pains."

The herb was first dedicated to Persephone and later, by the Christians, to St Peter, the guide to the souls of the dead. Of the mass of superstition associated with parsley, much concerns death or disaster. To be 'in need of parsley' meant hopelessly ill. The ancient Greeks believed the herb sprang from the blood of their mythological hero Archemorus, the forerunner of death, who was carelessly laid by his nurse on a bed of parsley and killed by serpents. The Greeks called it the herb of oblivion and made it into wreaths for graves and tombs, although, more cheerfully, Theocritus relates:

"At Sparta's Palace twenty beauteous mayds
The pride of Greece, fresh garlands crowned their heads
With hyacinths and twining parsley drest
Graced joyful Menelaus' marriage feast."

FECUNDITY

HOLLYHOCK — *Althaea rosea*

"The Holihock disdains the common size
Of Herbs, and like a tree do's proudly rise"
ABRAHAM COWLEY

The hollyhock was introduced to England from China in the sixteenth century and given the name holyoke by William Turner in
1548. Its other country names include: bysmalow, hock, hock-holler,
hollek and hollinhocke. It was used originally as a pot-herb but soon
became a garden favourite because of the beauty and varied colours of
its flowers, which look especially decorative in walled gardens. John
Lawrence wrote: "Proper places against walls or the corners of gardens
should be assigned to Hollyhocks where they can explain their beauty
to the distant views." It yields its seeds in prolific numbers, which
accounts for its meaning. The plant has a soothing effect on all parts of
the body and the flowers are useful medicinally in chest complaints.

FIDELITY IN ADVERSITY

WALLFLOWER — *Cheiranthus cheiri*

"The Wall-flower — the Wall-flower, how beautiful it blooms!
It gleams above the ruined tower, like sunlight over tombs;
It sheds a halo of repose around the wrecks of time —
To beauty give the flaunting rose, the Wall-flower is sublime."

DAVID MACBETH (DELTA) MOIR

Romance surrounds the wallflower. There is a touching story that, during the age of chivalry, a maiden who had been imprisoned in a Scottish castle attempted to escape and join her lover, but fell, alas, to the ground and died before his eyes, only to be reborn as this flower. Ever since, it has signified fidelity in adversity because it blooms in places where ruin and desolation prevail: in the cracks of walls of ancient castles, derelict cottages and crumbling tombstones.

"The rude stone fence, with fragrant wall-flow'rs gay"

FIDELITY IN LOVE
SPEEDWELL – *Veronica*

"Blue eyebright, loveliest flower that grows
In flower-loved England."
EBENEZER ELLIOTT

Also known as bird's-eye, cat's-eye, angel's-eye and eye of Christ, speedwell was named after St Veronica who, according to legend, was the compassionate woman on the road to Mount Calvary who wiped the sweat from Christ's brow as He laboured under the weight of His cross. The handkerchief she used was said to have been stamped with Christ's features and the petals of the speedwell which grew along the road. For her love and pity, Veronica was later canonized, and the flower itself became a token of woman's fidelity and fidelity in love. It was also used as a wound-herb and a cure for plague and leprosy.

"Around her hat a wreath was twined
Of blossoms blue as southern skies,
I asked their name and she replied:
'We call them Angel's eyes.'"

FLATTERY
VENUS'S LOOKING-GLASS – *Campanula speculum*

Also known as thimbles and Our Lady's gloves, this little flower was made the emblem of flattery in classical times because its brilliant corollas appeared to reflect the sun's rays like a mirror, and its round bloom resembled the circular-shaped looking-glasses of the period. There is also a story that Venus, on one of her rambles on earth, dropped a mirror that could beautify whatever it reflected. When a shepherd found it and gazed into it he, like Narcissus, fell in love with himself and promptly forgot his favourite nymph. Cupid, who discovered his mother's loss and was fearful of the consequences, broke the magic mirror and transformed the glittering fragments into these bright little flowers. In the eighteenth century Philip Miller mentions seventy-eight kinds of campanula, the best known of which today are the Canterbury bells and heath bells.

FOLLY

COLUMBINE — *Aquilegia vulgaris*

"The columbines, stone blue, or deep night brown,
Their honey-comb like blossoms hanging down;
Each cottage garden's fond adopted child,
Though heaths still claim them, where they yet grow wild."

JOHN CLARE

The name columbine derives from the Latin *columba*, a dove, because of extraordinary likeness of the spurred petals of each flower to a quintet of doves of pigeons displayed in a ring round the edge of a dish — a favourite device of ancient artists. However, the latin — *aquila* means 'like an eagle'. The plant was formerly called *Herba leonis*, from a belief that it was the favourite herb of the lion. It is made emblem of folly because of the rather peculiar shape of the nectaries, which turn over like the caps of old jesters. Columbine is under the dominion of Venus.

"Love is blind, and lovers cannot see
The pretty follies that themselves commit."

WILLIAM SHAKESPEARE

FOOLISHNESS

POMEGRANATE — *Punica granatum*

The pomegranate signifies foolishness because Proserpine was foolish enough to eat one in the underworld, with the result that she was forced to spend six months of the year in "the infernal regions" with Pluto. The great number of seeds contained in a single pomegranate has led to its being associated with fecundity, generation and wealth; there is also a belief that every pomegranate contains one seed which has come from Paradise. The pomegranate is frequently mentioned in the Bible and features predominantly in ancient art. It was introduced to England in 1596 by John Gerard. In the Mediterranean the plant is thought to give protection against evil spirits and the fallen blossoms are often threaded on necklaces and hung around the necks of children to alleviate stomach upsets. A syrup made from the seeds, Grenadine, is widely available today.

FORESIGHT

HOLLY – *Ilex aquifolium*

A holly hedge around a house or field was believed to keep out evil influences. It was protection against poison, the evil eye, storms and fire. Cows thrived if a sprig of Christmas holly was left in the cowshed. The custom of using holly as a Christmas decoration seems to stem from the Roman Saturnalia, celebrated in December. Folklore has it that elves and fairies join in the celebrations if they can shelter in the holly branches, in return for which they will protect the inhabitants from the antics of the house goblin. Medieval monks called it the Holy Tree and, as described in the carol "The Holly and the Ivy", the spines represent the Crown of Thorns, the white flowers purity and the birth of Christ, the red berries drops of blood, and the bitter bark the Passion. Legend has it that the holly first sprang up under the footsteps of Christ, when He trod the earth. Almost all parts of the holly have been used for healing purposes. Folklore has a barbaric-sounding cure for chilblains – thrashing the affected areas with holly twigs.

FORGET-ME-NOT

MOUSE-EAR SCORPION GRASS – *Myosotis palustris*

The name scorpion grass was introduced by the first-century Greek authority, Dioscorides, because of the flower's coiled stems. The term forget-me-not came to the fore much later, appearing throughout Europe in nineteenth-century sonnets and particularly in German love songs. Coleridge uses the name in his poem, 'The Keepsake'. It was used as a simple charm: "Think of the one you wish to be thinking of you when you pull a sprig of forget-me-not, and you will immediately have a place in his – or her – thoughts. Plant forget-me-not on a grave, and, however dry the soil, as long as you live the plant will never die." The French name, *ne m'oubliez pas*, refers to the tale of the Knight Roland, who, while strolling by the river-side with his lady, stretched to pick the flowers and fell in. The weight of his armour was so great that he was unable to escape, but, before drowning, he threw the flowers to her feet, calling out the poignant words – forget-me-not – that have been associated with them ever since.

FORSAKEN

LILAC – *Syringa*

"How slowly through the lilac-scented air
Descends the tranquil moon!"
HENRY WADSWORTH LONGFELLOW

The name derives from the Persian *lilak*, "bluish plant or flower", and it was in Persia that the custom originated of presenting a spray of lilac to a lover as a sensitive way of indicating that the romance had died. An American superstition has it that a girl who wears lilac is destined to remain unmarried – this was inspired by the story of an English nobleman who seduced an innocent girl and then abandoned her, leaving her to die of a broken heart. Overnight the wreath of purple lilac left on her grave turned white, the symbol of innocence and mourning. On account of the purity and brief duration of its beautiful flowers, the white lilac is often presented as the emblem of youth.

"The Lilac various in array, now white,
Now sanguine, and her beauteous head now set
With purple spikes pyramidal, as if
Studious of ornament, yet unresolved
Which hue she most approved, she chose them all."
WILLIAM COWPER

Gerard, however, found the white lilac of "a pleasante and sweete smell, but in my judgment *too sweete*, troubling and molesting the head in a very strange manner. I once gathered the flowers and laid them in my chamber windowe, whiche smelled more strongly after they had been together a few howers, with such a ponticke and unacquainted savour, that they awaked me from sleepe, so that I could not take any rest till I had cast them out of my chamber." It is perhaps because of this overpowering fragrance that it is considered unlucky in England and Scotland to bring lilac, especially the *Syringa alba*, into the house; it is considered a flower of death, presaging misfortune and is often laid on coffins:

"Here, coffin that slowly passes,
I give you my sprig of lilac."
WALT WHITMAN

FRIENDSHIP
and PLEASURE OF MEMORY
PERIWINKLE − *Vinca*

Vinca was a familiar plant to Chaucer, who referred to it as "the fresh Pervinke rich of hew". In France, where it was also known as virgin flower, it was considered the emblem of the pleasures of memory and sincere friendship – perhaps in allusion, originally, to Rousseau's fond recollection of his friend Madame de Warens, prompted, after thirty years, by the sight of the periwinkle in flower, which they had once admired together. Also known as cockles and sorceror's violet, it used to be customary to place garlands of it on the biers of dead children, which is why it is known as the flower of death in Italy. Medicinally, it has been used to treat a wide variety of complaints, including nightmares, hysteria, diarrhoea, haemorrhages, scurvy and inflamed tonsils. Culpeper tells us it "stays bleeding at the mouth and nose, if it be chewed" and Albartus Magnus reports that "Perwynke when it is beate unto powder with wormes of ye earth wrapped about it and with an herbe called houslyke, it induceth love between man and wyfe if it be used in their meales."

FRUGALITY
CHICORY OR ENDIVE − *Cichorium endivia*

"A garden-sallad,
Of endive, radishes, and succory."
JOHN DRYDEN

Chicory, or succory as it was more generally named, was used quite extensively by the Romans. The Elizabethans used it cosmetically, making up a drink which was taken to clear spotty skins; it was also prescribed for jaundice, liver and spleen complaints. In 1788 Arthur Young recommended its use as cattle feed. The leaf was believed to give the bearer the power of invisibility. The plant also had the ability to open locked chests, though this could be done only on St James's Day, 25 July. It was essential to use a golden knife, while holding a chicory leaf against the lock. The lock-picker had to work in silence, however, for if he spoke, he would surely die.

GALLANTRY

S W E E T W I L L I A M – *Dianthus barbatus*

"And the borders filled with daisies and pied sweet Williams
And busy pansies; and there as we gazed and dreamed
And breathed the swooning smell of the packed carnations
The present was always the crown of all it seemed."

ROBERT BRIDGES

Also known as sweet John, tolmeiner, London tuft, bloomy-down, pride of London, the sweet William belongs to the same family as the clove carnation. Parkinson refers to the use of nineteen varieties in medicine, which were said to have tonic properties and were used internally and externally to allay the bites and stings of poisonous insects and snakes.

"Sweet William small has form and aspect bright
Like that sweet flower that yields great Jove delight."

ABRAHAM COWLEY

GENEROSITY

ORANGE – *Citrus sinensis*

The orange is associated with generosity and "great fullness" because of its unusual ability to produce fruit, flowers and foliage all at the same time. The Virgin Mary is said to have plucked three oranges from a tree, presided over by a sleeping eagle, to feed herself, the infant Jesus and Joseph, and in Sicily statues of the Madonna are decorated with orange boughs on Easter Sunday. In Victorian times on Boxing Day the people of Brighton used to bowl oranges along the streets. Both Milton and Spenser believed that the orange was the "golden apple" presented by Juno to Jupiter on the day of their marriage. It was one of the labours of Hercules to obtain some of these golden apples of the Hesperides. Milton alludes to the orange as a tree:

> *"Whose fruit, burnished with golden rind,*
> *Hung amiable, Hesperian fables true,*
> *If true, here only, and of delicious taste."*

GENIUS
PLANE TREE – *Platanus*

"His spreading planes their pleasant shade extend."
VIRGIL

The broad plane tree is made emblem of genius because it once shaded the philosophers of Athens. In Plato's time philosophers used to walk and converse under the shade of these delightful trees. The plane was held sacred to Helen, the wife of Menelaus. In Greece, when lovers are obliged to separate, they exchange, as a pledge of fidelity, the halves of a leaf of the plane. When they meet again each one produces their half-leaf, fitting them together to confirm they have been faithful while apart.

GLORY
BAY – *Laurus nobilis* or LAUREL – *Prunus laurocerasus*

*"Fame's bright star and glory's swell
By the glossy leaf of the Bay are given."*
JAMES GATES PERCIVAL

As Apollo's symbol, wreaths of bay and laurel were used to crown victors and heroes (both in games and war), as well as philosophers, poets and orators – it is from such a practice that the title Poet Laureate derives. In Greek mythology, the nymph Daphne, desired and pursued by Apollo, fled from his advances and was changed into a bay tree. It was thought to have powers to protect against evil, guard man's social well-being and confer the gifts of culture, music, song and poetry. Culpeper was a great advocate of bay: "Neither witch nor devil, nor thunder or lightning will hurt a man in a place where a Bay Tree is." Describing how much bay meant to his countrymen in Tudor times, Parkinson wrote, "They serve both for pleasure and profit, both for ornament and use, both for honest civil uses and for physic, yea both for the sick and for the fecund, both for the living and the dead." If a bay tree died it was considered an awful omen of death and disaster. Shakespeare refers to this belief in *Richard* II: "'Tis thought the King is dead: we will not stay, the bay trees in our country are all wither'd."

A GOOD EDUCATION

CHERRY — *Prunus cerasus*

"Cherries on the ryse |twig|"
FIFTEENTH CENTURY LONDON STREET CRY

According to Pliny, in the year 75 BC Lucullus brought cherry trees from Cerasus, in Pontus, after his victory over Mithridates VI and "within 120 years cherry trees had crossed the sea as far as Britain". Culpeper says, "The gum of the cherry tree dissolved in wine is good for colds, coughs and hoarseness of the throat; mends the colour of the faces, sharpens the eye sight and provokes appetite, and dissolved, the water thereof is of much use to break the stone and to expel gravel and wind." William Cole says of the fruit: "They strengthen and stir up appetite to meat. A tisane of the stalks has astringent and pectoral properties and makes a pleasant beverage." It is said that Christ gave a Cherry to St Peter, cautioning him at the same time not to despise little things, to pay attention to detail, and hence its meaning. In Hamburg a Feast of Cherries commemorates the liberation of the town from the Hussites in 1432 - the children were sent, dressed in black, to plead with the enemy, who promised to spare the city and sent the children home with their arms full of the fruit.

GOSSIP

COBOEA — *Coboea scandens*

"Go to a gossip's feast, and goude with me.
— With all my heart, I'll gossip at this feast."
WILLIAM SHAKESPEARE

This climbing shrub from Central and South America is known as the cup-and-saucer plant simply because the petals and sepals of its large, showy flowers resemble cups and saucers. The tea table is the scene of much innocent chit-chat and because of this and the fact that the flower has long, wagging, tongue-like tendrils, it has come to symbolize gossip. Like a gossip, the tendrils latch on to everything they meet and run from branch to branch, spreading fast.

GRACEFULNESS
PELARGONIUM (WHITE) – *Pelargonium*

"Grace was in her steps, heav'n in her eye,
In every gesture dignity and love."
JOHN MILTON

The 250 or so species of pelargonium are found throughout tropical areas. Introduced from South Africa in the eighteenth century, they were at their most popular in Britain in the Victorian era. They flower very freely and are, indeed, graceful, as is emphasized by some of the species names: L'elegante, Queen of Denmark, and Madame Salleroi. The scent is not apparent until the foliage is rubbed or bruised, when it becomes very strong, ranging from a fragrance of roses to peppermint, nutmeg or citron. An oil, extracted from the leaves, is widely used as a substitute for rose oil and more costly essences in 'rose' soaps, shampoos and toilet waters. The leaf of *Pelargonium capitatum* gives a pleasant flavour to milk puddings, jams and jellies.

GRANDEUR

BEECH − *Fagus*

"Mixt with huge Oaks, as next in rank and state,
Their kindred Beech and Cerris claim a seat."

RENÉ RAPIN

The beech is a grand, abundant tree, providing ample shade from the scorching sun or shelter from a shower. According to Lucian, beech trees as well as the sacred oak were the medium through which the Oracles of Jupiter at Dodona were delivered. A large part of the Greek ship, *Arga*, was built of beech and certain beams in the vessel gave oracles to the Argonauts, warning them of approaching calamities. It was from the top of two beech trees that Minerva and Apollo, in the form of vultures, watched the fight between the Greeks and the Trojans. Wine was drunk from beech-wood bowls. Pliny wrote that its wood should never be cut for fuel and, as a tree of good augury, specially favoured, it was believed to be exempt from lightning.

HATRED

BASIL – *Ocymum basilium*

"The basil-tuft that waves
Its fragrant blossom over graves."

Despite its delicious culinary qualities, basil has, over the centuries, aroused the most extraordinary passions. It was a herb surrounded by acrimony. To the ancient Greeks it represented hatred and misfortune, and they illustrated poverty as a pitiful woman in ragged clothes with basil at her side. They believed the herb would not grow unless the seeds were sown to the accompaniment of a barrage of curses and abuse and the Romans, too, believed basil needed to be reviled to flourish. Its reputation went before it into France, where *semer le basilic* (scatter the basil) was a popular, slanderous expression. On the plus side, it was considered proof against witches; in Italy it was a love token, believed to have such power that if a man accepted a shoot of fresh basil from a woman, his love for her would be undying, and in Crete it symbolized "love washed with tears". In Tudor England, little pots of bush basil were often given as graceful compliments by farmers' wives to visitors. In India, its native land, it is revered as a plant of great holiness: it is the herb of Vishnu, Krishna and Siva, and is found around Hindu temples, and placed upon the dead. But its unpleasant associations persisted. Superstition had it that a sprig of basil laid under a pot would breed a scorpion and a French physician, Hilarius, claimed that an acquaintance of his "by common smelling to it, had a scorpion breed in his brain". Culpeper, too, had his doubts about basil. "Something is the matter," he wrote. "This herb and rue will not grow together, no, nor near one another, and we know rue is as great an enemy to poison as any that grows." Recently, however, basil has left its black past behind and become an extremely popular ingredient, particularly in pasta sauces and as an accompaniment to a tomato and mozzarella salad. Basil's distinctive flavour was responsible for making "Fetter Lane sausages" famous.

"Herbs too, she knew, and well of each could speak
That in her garden sipp'd the silv'ry dew; . . .
The tufted basil, pun-provoking thyme,
Fresh balm, and mary-gold of cheerful hue."

WILLIAM SHENSTONE

HAUGHTINESS
S U N F L O W E R — *Helianthus annuus*

"The sunflower turns on her god when he sets
The same look which she did when he rose."
THOMAS MOORE

The sunflower is a native of South America and Peru, where it was once an emblem of the Sun God of the Incas. The Spanish invaders found exquisite representations of the sunflower, wrought in gold, in the Inca temples. Its meaning may have arisen because the plant can grow to a great height and has a rather exalted look. Gerard claimed he grew flowers 40cms (16ins) across on stems of 4m (14ft); but he was trumped by Crispin de Pass, who reported that "sown in the Royal Garden at Madrid in Spain, they grew to 24 feet in height; but at Padua in Italy it is written they attained to the height of 40 feet". Sunflower seeds make an excellent oil; they can also be roasted like coffee beans, ground and made into a drink. The flowers contain a yellow dye and the dried leaves can be used in place of tobacco.

HEARTLESSNESS
or a BOASTER
H Y D R A N G E A — *Hydrangea hortensis*

"No more delays, vain boaster! but begin,
I prophesy before hand I shall win:
I'll teach you how to brag another time."
JOHN DRYDEN

A native of China and Japan, the hydrangea was introduced to England in 1740. As it gives out such magnificent blossoms without ever producing fruit, it was likened to a boaster, for just as the latter's vaunting words are vacuous, so the large, showy flowers develop into nothing of substance. It was named by Gronovius, a Dutch writer, who derived the name from the Greek words *hudor* for water and *aggeion* for jar or vessel, because it is a marsh plant and needs a good deal of water. Most commonly cultivated for its beauty, the hydrangea also has medicinal uses for bladder and kidney complaints.

89

HEEDLESSNESS

ALMOND – *Prunus amygdalis*

The almond was made emblem of heedlessness because the tree blossoms early without the protection of foliage. Its Hebrew name is *shakad*, awakening. Aaron's rod, which budded and brought forth in the tabernacle all in one day, was said in the Bible to be of an almond tree. It is called *Phylla* by the Greeks in reference to the legend of Phyllis, a Thracian queen, who died of grief and was turned into an almond tree when her husband, Demophon, failed to return to her from the Trojan war. At length Demophon did return and, devastated by his loss, clasped the tree in his arms, whereupon it burst into bloom out of sheer happiness. Virgil wrote:

> *"With many a bud, if flowering Almonds bloom,*
> *And arch their gay festoons that breathe perfume,*
> *So shall thy harvest like profusion yield,*
> *And cloudless suns mature the fertile field."*

HONESTY

HONESTY – *Lunaria*

There is a popular belief that wherever the purple honesty is found flourishing, its owner is of a particularly honest disposition. Certainly, money is associated with honesty because its bells hang like open purses by the side of its stem, and it sometimes goes by the country name of money-in-both-pockets. Other old names include silks and satins, silver plate and white satin, which refer to the transparent seed vessels that remain when the seeds are scattered. It was also called lunary and moonwort because of the disc-like shape of its seed pods. The plant was credited with magical properties and used in incantations and charms as it was purported to have the "power of putting monsters to flight".

"Enchanting Lunary here lies,
In sorcerie excelling."
MICHAEL DRAYTON

HOPE

HAWTHORN — *Cratægus*

"Mark the faire blooming of the Hawthorne tree,
Who, finely clothed in a robe of white
Fills full the wanton eye with May's delight."

WILLIAM BROWNE

Hawthorn is one of the oldest plants known to man. An emblem of hope and a tree of good augury for the Greeks, it was also the symbol of fertility and May blossoms were used in wedding festivities. The newlywed couple used to be escorted to the bridal bed with lighted torches made of hawthorn wood. In olden times May Day celebrations centred round the hawthorn, which was later replaced by the garlanded maypole – both symbolized the transition into fertile summer. Superstition surrounds it. In Suffolk the first person to find a branch in full blossom was rewarded with a celebratory dish of cream. Girls would bathe their faces in hawthorn dew at first dawn on May Day in the hope that it would make them beautiful. The tree was said to ward off lightning. Yet many people still believe it is unlucky to bring the blossom into the house.

HOPELESS and HEARTLESS

LOVE-LIES-BLEEDING — *Amaranthus caudatus*

"True love lies bleeding, with the hearts at ease;
And golden rods, and tansy running high
That o'er the pale top, smiled on passers by."

JOHN CLARE

Love-lies-bleeding is also known as flower of love, velvet flower, red-cockscomb, balder herb, floramor, flower gentle and, in Devon, as prince's feather, although in Sussex this name refers to London pride. It originated in tropical Africa and South America and was important to the Aztecs, who used its seed for food and for ceremonial purposes. Known as Inca wheat, eighteen of the Aztec empire's granaries were once filled with its tiny seeds. It has showy tassels of red flowers, which no doubt encouraged both the plant's name and emblem.

HOSPITALITY
OAK – *Quercus*

Oak apples (a gall) and leaves are traditionally worn on 29 May to honour King Charles II, who, to avoid capture, hid in an oak tree at Boscobel, Shropshire, after the battle of Worcester. The 'hospitable' tree's pale-grey bark, thick and deeply fissured, provides a refuge for all kinds of insects and at least 500 species of invertebrates use the bark, wood, or leaves in Britain. It features prominently in folklore and European mythology, in which it is worshipped for its human qualities such as the haunting shrieks and groans it emits when felled. (Its hard wood became the most important timber for ships - the British "hearts of oak".) Particular reverence was paid to individual oaks by Druids, who held the oak sacred. It had a wide range of magical powers. It gave protection from lightning; a nail driven into the trunk cured toothache; and merely to carry an acorn preserved youth.

HUMANITY
or BENEFICENCE
MALLOW (OR MARSH MALLOW) – *Althœa officinalis*

The ancient Romans had some variety of mallow served us as a vegetable and the Egyptians, Syrians and Chinese also used them as food. In the time of Job, the plants were eaten by wandering tribes who, he says "cut up Mallows by the bushes, and Juniper-roots for their meat". The seeds of the mallow look remarkably like cheese and in Yorkshire are known as fairy cheeses. Clare recalls the days of his childhood, when he and his playmates sat:

> "Picking from Mallows sport to please,
> The crumpled seed we call'd a cheese."

Mallow was said to have many healing properties and Pliny wrote, "Whosoever shall take a spoonful of any of the Mallows shall that day be free from all diseases that may come unto him." He also believed the plant to be effective against "the falling sickness" and for exciting the passions.

HUMILITY

Broom – *Spartium*

Broom made its first official heraldic appearance on the great seal of Richard I when he became king in 1189. His family name, Planta-genet, was taken from *Planta genista*, the broom's medieval name; the motto beneath it on the seal was *Deus exaltat humiles* (God exalteth the lowly). In Italy, too, it was symbolic of humility: legend states it was accursed and humiliated for having made such a noise in the garden of Gethsemene while Christ was praying there that His persecutors were able to surprise him. Broom is supposed to have been beloved by witches. In Germany it was used for decorations on Whit Sunday and also as a charm; in France it was grown for feeding sheep. Wild broom blooms in England in April, May and June and if it has plenty of flowers it is said to be a sign of a bumper grain crop. The six-times-married Henry VIII – a far from humble king – was "wont to drink the distilled water of Broome-floures, against surfets and diseases thereof arising".

IDLENESS

ICE PLANT — *Mesembryanthemum crystallinum*

*"The amomum there with intermingling flowers
And cherries hangs her twigs — Geranium boasts
Her crimson honours, and the spangled beau,
Ficoides glitters bright the winter long."*

WILLIAM COWPER

Mesembryanthemum derives from the Greek, meaning "middle-of-the-day flower". It is also known as diamond, ficoides, fig marigold, hottentot fig and viggie and called ice plant because of its icy, crystalline appearance. An exotic, succulent plant, the mesembryanthemum's purple, pink or yellow flowers open only in the heat of midday, promoting the suggestion of idleness. Ice plant also infers "Your looks freeze me", and certainly it can glitter like diamonds, encouraging the idea of icicles in the cold hearts of those who never warm to friendship.

IMMORTALITY

AMARANTH — *Amaranthus*

"Immortal Amaranth! a flower which once
In Paradise, fast by the Tree of Life,
Began to bloom; but soon for Man's offence,
To Heaven removed."

JOHN MILTON

The amaranth was sacred to the Greeks and Romans. An everlasting plant, its name means 'never fading' and 'incorruptible', hence it was made emblem of immortality. Its ability to revive its shape and colour when wet was much used by the Greeks and Romans for winter chaplets. They classed it as a funeral flower, placing it on their tombs, and Homer describes the Thessalians as wearing crowns of amaranths at the funeral of Achilles. It also retains its beauty when dried and so is frequently used as decoration. Love and friendship are also signified by the amaranth. The Swedish order of the Knights of the Amaranth was instituted by Queen Christiana in 1653. At the end of a ball, she stripped herself of diamonds, distributed them to the company, and presented the new order of knighthood, consisting of a ribbon and a medal with an amaranth in enamel surrounded by the motto:

Dolce nella memoria

Also known as prince's feather, love-lies-bleeding, fox's-tail and Flora-more, Gerard wrote of it in the sixteenth century: "It farre exceedeth my skil to describe the beautie and excellencie of this rare plant, called *Floramore*, and I think the pensill of the most curious painter will be at a staie when he shall come to set him downe in his liuely colours." Culpeper, following The Doctrine of Signatures, prescribed amaranth (or love-lies-bleeding) to "stop all fluxes of blood." He wrote, "The flowers dried and beaten into powder stops the terms in women, and so do almost all other red things."

"Sad Amaranthus, made a flower but late,
Sad Amaranthus, in whose purple gore
Me seems I see Amintas wretched fate,
To whom sweet poets verse hath given endless date."

EDMUND SPENSER

IMPATIENCE

BALSAM (RED) — *Impatiens balsamina*

"Balsam, with its shaft of amber."

To the Turks, this flower represents ardent love because of the way, as maturity approaches, the slightest touch causes the plant to dart out its seeds spontaneously: hence also its generic name, *Impatiens*, and its English appellation touch me not. John Gerard stated that the plant was highly esteemed for its ability to alleviate the pains of childbirth; he also said that it was considered a valuable agent in curing sterility – the patient had first to bathe in and then anoint himself with an oil compounded with the fruit.

*"Why, Sir, if you were to read
Richardson for the story, your
impatience would be so much fretted
that you would hang yourself."*
SAMUEL JOHNSON

IMPERFECTION

HENBANE — *Hyoscyamus niger*

*"And I ha' been plucking, plants among
Hemlock, Henbane, Adders-tongue."*
BEN JONSON

This baneful plant, whose literal meaning is 'hen-killer' or 'hen-death', signifies imperfection because its medicinal properties are outweighed by its dangerous qualities. It was one of the ancient lethal herbs sought out by witches to use in potions and has a mysterious reputation. Douce wrote "Henbane, called *insana*, mad, for the use thereof is perillous, for if it be eate or dronke, it breedeth madness, or slowe lykeness of sleep." "The whole plant," wrote Culpeper, "hath a very ill, odoriferous smell." Gerard said that merely to smell the flowers brought about heavy sleep. Hyoscyamine, used in "twilight sleep" in childbirth, is obtained from the leaves and plant tops and still used today. (This was the drug Crippen used to murder his wife in a famous case at the beginning of this century.)

INGRATITUDE

Y ELLOW G ENTIAN − *Gentiana lutea* and C ROWFOOT − *Ranunuculus*

"See how the giant spires of yellow bloom of the sun loving Gentian,
in the heat are shining on those naked slopes like flame."

The gentian is named after Gentius, King of Illyria, who first discovered the medicinal virtues of this bitter plant. Legend has it that
it was revealed as a cure for plague to Ladislaus one time king of
Hungary. He shot an arrow into the air, praying that it should be
guided towards some herb which might alleviate the plight of his
people, who were suffering from a pestilence that was ravaging the
country. The arrow plunged into the heart of a gentian plant, which
proved a cure for plague. It is made emblem of ingratitude because it
proves such a challenge to cultivate, demanding great care and
patience. Crowfoot, also known as devil's buttercup or poison cup, has
the same meaning because it insinuates itself into pastures and is
poisonous to cattle.

INJUSTICE

Hop – *Humulus lupulus*

Hops were made the emblem of injustice because they were treated as noxious weeds until the sixteenth century, when their true value in the brewing of beer was recognized.

> *"The hop for his profit, I thus do exalt*
> *It strengtheneth drink and it flavoureth malt:*
> *And being well brewed long kept it will last,*
> *And drawing abide if ye draw not too fast."*

In feudal times hops were part of small tithes, or taxes, which the peasantry had to pay. King Vladimar of Russia, in AD 985, when signing a peace treaty with the Bulgars, swore to abide by it till stone swam on the water, or hop leaves sank to the bottom. It is a very old custom in Russia to cover the head of a bride with hop leaves to signify joy, abundance and intoxication.

INNOCENCE

D A I S Y — *Bellis perennis*

"A very pearl of flowers indeed
This little firstling of the mead;
So innocent it is, so sweet,
It bears the name of 'Marguerite';
The poets call it 'eye of day,'
'Daisy' the children fondly say:
Thus pretty Bellis still we see
Dancing right gaily in the lee;
Emblem of innocence is she."

The daisy, with its "simplicity and unaffected air", is the flower of innocence. Together with the buttercup, it is one of the first flowers of childhood, evoking memories of daisy-spangled lawns, making daisy chains and plucking the petals off while chanting fortune-telling rhymes. Well within a baby's grasp, daisies are never taboo to touch like so many other flowers, which has led to them being called bairnwort. There are many legends connected with the daisy: she was a nymph changed into the flower to escape the amorous embrace of Vertumnus; she was Chaucer's "goode Alceste", who was turned into a "daisie". The daisy is the flower of the newborn and especially of babies who die – they are said to scatter daisies on the earth to comfort their parents, as Malvina was comforted after the death of her infant son Oscar by seeing daisies appear on the hills of Cromla. Chaucer calls it "the eie of daie", no doubt because it closes its petals at night and during rainy weather. It was lucky to step on the first daisy of the year. Some say spring has not arrived until you can put your foot upon twelve daisies at once. Alphonse Karr wrote "There is a plant that no insect, no animal attacks – that ornament of the field, with golden disc and rays of silver, spreading in such profusion at our feet: nothing is so humble, nothing is so much respected." Putting daisy roots under a pillow was said to prompt pleasant dreams of loved ones, and placing a daisy flower into the left foot of a stocking promoted the possibility of pregnancy.

"All beneath th' unrivalled rose
The lowly Daisy sweetly blows."
ROBERT BURNS

INSPIRATION

ANGELICA — *Angelica archangelica*

"My fancy form'd thee of angelic kind."
ALEXANDER POPE

According to one legend, angelica was revealed in a dream by an angel to cure the plague. The story lent the plant a holy quality; it was considered an infallible guard against sorcery and incantations and it became known as *Angelica archangelica* or The Holy Ghost, because it bloomed on the day of Michael the Archangel, 8 May. Angelica's reputation as a medicinal plant dates back to prehistoric times and was inevitably linked with superstitious, pagan beliefs, which persisted in early Christian minds. It was considered a complete protection against infectious diseases – Gerard recommended a piece of the root held in the mouth to drive away pestilential air – and an antidote to poisonous bites, especially from mad dogs. Concerned parents were advised to mix the dried and powdered roots with wine to "abate the raging lust in young persons."

INSTABILITY

DAHLIA — *Dahlia*

"Beauty clothes the fragrant air,
The Dahlia will each glory wear,
With tints as bright and leaves as green."
THEODORE MARTIN

The dahlia is named after the Swedish botanist Andreas Dahl (1751-89) but came originally from Mexico. Its first appearance in Europe coincided with the French Revolution and the plants perished and were lost. The second introduction coincided with Napoleon being made Emperor of France and it was from these incidents that the dahlia was chosen as the symbol of instability. The tubers contain insulin and were given to diabetics. Dr Dahl originally hoped that the dahlia would gain in popularity as a vegetable rather than as a garden flower, but it never rivalled the potato and he died disappointed, although by the 1800s in Britain the dahlia was "the most fashionable flower in the country".

INTELLECT

Walnut – *Juglans nigra*

"The walnut then approach'd, more large and tall,
His fruit, which we a nut, the Gods an acorn call."

Abraham Cowley

The walnut became associated with intellect because of its resemblance to the brain. For this reason it was deemed a good tonic for the brain and an excellent hair restorer! Gerard wrote that "the green and tender nuts boiled in sugar and eaten as 'suckarde' are a most pleasant and delectable sweetmeat to comfort the stomach". Walnut trees were well established in Henry VIII's great palace in 1665, as Samuel Pepys records on 21 September (at the height of the Great Plague): "To Nonsuch, to the Exchequer by appointment, and walked up and down the house and park . . ./ a great walk of an elme and a walnutt set one after another in order". The tree was also considered unlucky and a haunt of witches.

JOY

WOOD-SORREL — *Oxalis acetosella*

"The cresses on the water and the Sorrell is at hand,
And the cuckoo's calling clearly his note of music bland."
SAMUEL FERGUSON

Wood-sorrel was known in the sixteenth century as alleluya and panis-cuculi (cuckoo's meat) "either," wrote Gerard, "because the cuckowe feedeth thereon, or by reason, when it flowereth, the cuckowe singeth most, as whiche time also 'Alleluya' was woont to be sang in churches" – that is, at Easter. It was also known as God's bread, stub-wort and wood sower, candle-of-the-woods and bird's bannock. It is through this connection with birds and song that its meaning derives. Sorrel can be added to salads, soups and sauces and old herbalists used it to treat a great number of illnesses, including stomach aches, sore throats, boils, ringworm and scurvy. A juice made from the leaves was used as a gargle to treat mouth ulcers.

JUSTICE
or RENDER ME JUSTICE
CHESTNUT — *Castanea sativa*

"A woman's tongue,
That gives not half so great a blow to th' ear,
As will a chestnut in a farmer's fire."
WILLIAM SHAKESPEARE

The chestnut was classed by Pliny among the fruit trees on account of the value of the nut as an item of food. The chestnuts of Asia Minor supplied Xenophon's whole army with food as the men retreated along the borders of the Euxine. It flourished in Europe and in 1573 Thomas Tusser listed it as an essential fruit in a good Tudor garden. The *castagno dei cento cavalli* (chestnut of the hundred horses) upon Mount Etna is said to be more than 200 feet in circumference. It is included in the list of funereal trees and chestnuts are eaten with solemnity in Italy on saints' days. In some houses they are left on the table in the belief that the deceased poor will come during the night and feast on them. John Evelyn said they were "delicacies for princes and a lusty and masculine food for rusticks."

KNIGHT ERRANTRY
MONK'S HOOD OR HELMET-FLOWER — *Aconitum napellus*

This little yellow flower is surrounded by a whorl of glossy, green, deeply cut leaves, which inspired the name helmet-flower and encouraged the association with knight errantry. John Gerard wrote, "It groweth upon the mountaines of Germanie; we haue great quantitie of it in our London gardens. It bloweth in Ianuarie: the seed is ripe in the end of March." It contains a virulent poison and was used to tip the ends of arrow-heads used in war or for hunting wild animals.

"The ancient errant knights
Won all their mistresses in fights:
They cut whole giants into fritters,
To put them into am'rous twitters."
HUDIBRAS

LAMENTATION
ASPEN TREE – *Populus tremula*

The Bretons have a legend that the Saviour's cross was made of aspen wood, and that the ceaseless trembling of the leaves of this tree marks the shuddering of horror at the Crucifixion. However, there is an old German belief that, during their flight into Egypt, the Holy Family came to a dense forest, in which, but for an angelic guide, they would have lost their way. As they entered this wilderness all the trees bowed down in reverence to the infant God; only the aspen, in her exceeding pride and arrogance, refused to acknowledge Him and stood upright:

> *"Only the Aspen stands erect and free,*
> *Scorning to join the voiceless worship pure;*
> *But see! He casts one look upon the tree,*
> *Struck to the heart she trembles evermore!"*
> ROBERT HENDERSON

(An old European saying compares the leaves with women's wagging tongues.)

LASTING BEAUTY
STOCK OR GILLIFLOWER – *Matthiola incana*

> *"The white and purple Gilliflowers that stay*
> *In blossom – lingering summer half away."*
> JOHN CLARE

Lasting beauty is represented by the stock, whose charm, although less graceful than the rose or the lily, is more durable. One of the first garden flowers cultivated in England (and said to have also grown in Paradise), its popularity endures today and it can be seen growing in fragrant profusion in cottage and formal gardens alike. They were certainly common during Elizabethan times, for Gerard tells us that the plant was "greatly esteemed for the beauty of its flowers and pleasant sweet perfume". He mentioned that "stock gillofloures do grow in most gardens in England".

LASTING PLEASURE
SWEET PEA – *Lathyrus odoratus*

"Here are Sweet-Peas on tip-toe for flight,
With wings of gentle flush, o'er delicate white,
And taper fingers catching at all things
To bind them all about with tiny rings."

JOHN KEATS

The sweet pea arrived in England in 1699 when Abbé Cupani of Sicily sent some seed of a new plant to Dr Uvedale, his friend in London. These small, fragrant flowers, peculiar for their elegant negligence of shape, delicacy and richness of colouring, became steadily more popular and by 1837 Messrs J. Carter & Co. of Holborn, London were offering a wide range of seeds. They were particularly popular in Edwardian times and a great favourite with Queen Alexandra. They were made emblem of lasting pleasure because the blossoms constantly renew themselves and because of their fragrant perfume.

LIFE

L u c e r n e — *Medicago sativa*

"Life is sweet."

Lucerne grows wild in Cornwall and other parts of England, where it is known by the country names of St Maw's clover, spotted clover, purple medicle or purple grass. It has also been called lucifer, medick, sanfoin, snail clover and Burgundy hay. The Romans cultivated it as a crop and in China, under the name of Mu su, it has been grown since the second century BC. Tradition states that it was brought to China by General Chang Chien of the Han dynasty. It is one of the best foods for cattle and is equally nourishing for man, which is perhaps why it was made the symbol of life. It can also flourish in poor soil and produces three crops a year from the same roots. It is used as a tonic for the brain and spinal chord and is taken to regulate weight. The roots of the black medick are said to make good tooth powder. In America lucerne is known as alfalfa.

LIGHTHEARTEDNESS

SHAMROCK

The shamrock, from the Irish *seamrog*, "little clover", has become the national emblem of Ireland and is traditionally worn on St Patrick's Day, 17 March. Legend states that St Patrick, on an evangelizing mission in Ireland, illustrated the doctrine of Three in One and One in Three of the Trinity with a shamrock and his audience immediately accepted Christianity. Before then, the shamrock had been used as a pagan charm against witches and fairies, who were supposed to be especially active around 17 March, which was taken to be the end of winter and the beginning of spring. Edmund Spenser, in his *View of the Present State of Ireland* (*c*.1597-8) wrote of famine-stricken Irishmen after the wars in Munster: "And yf they founde a plotte of water-cresses or shamrokes, there they flocked as to a feast for the time." In parts of Ireland "shamrock bread" is made from the flowers and pods.

LIGHTNESS

LARKSPUR – *Delphineum ajacis*

The larkspur is supposed to have sprung from the blood of Ajax and in floral language is made emblem of lightness because of the graceful airiness of the flowers. They are found widely in Britain and over much of the United States. Also known as lark's-head, lark's-toes, lark's-claw, knight's-spur, Jacob's ladder, and delphinium from its supposed likeness to the spur of a dolphin's head. Gerard wrote in the sixteenth century, "For the flowers and especially before they are perfected have a certaine shewe and likeness of those Dolphines, which old pictures and armes of certaine ancient families have expressed with a crooked and bending figure or shape by whiche signe also the Heavenlie Dolphine is set foorth." They have been cultivated since the time of the Pharoahs, when their importance was entirely due to the supposed ability of the seeds to destroy vermin. It was also believed that if it was thrown at a scorpion or snake the creature would not be able to move or have the strength to sting until the plant was taken away. The expressed juice of the petals, with a little alum added, makes an excellent blue ink.

LOVE FLOWERS

*"Who that has loved knows not the tender tale
Which flowers reveal, when lips are coy to tell?"*
EDWARD GEORGE EARLE BULWER-LYTTON

Flowers are often used to express love in all its many forms. The carnation, so tradition has it, sprang from the graves of lovers and means "Alas for my poor heart"; the myrtle is the classical flower of love, but it is the rose, with its contrasts of sharp thorns and delicate velvety scented flowers – a mixture of pain and pleasure – that has come to symbolize true love, which survives happiness and misfortune alike. Floral language has played a significant role in courtship and marriage rituals since earliest times and continues today. The word 'posy' was originally the name given to a poem which, in a more romantic age, accompanied the gift of a bouquet to a loved one. Here is a list of flowers of love:

Acacia   *Chaste love*
Acacia, Yellow   *Secret love*
Ambrosia   *Love returned*
Carnation, Pink   *Woman's love*
Catchfly, Red   *Youthful love*
Chrysanthemum, Red   *I love*
Chrysanthemum, Yellow   *Slighted love*
Cinquefoil   *Beloved daughter*
Coreopsis, Arkansa   *Love at first sight*
Forget-me-Not   *True love*
Heliotrope   *Eternal love*
Honey Flower   *Love sweet and secret*
Honeysuckle   *Bonds of love*
Indian Pink, Double   *Always lovely*
Ivy   *Conjugal love*
Lemon Blossom   *Fidelity in love*
Lilac, Purple   *First emotions of love*
Linden or Lime Tree   *Conjugal love*
Lotus Flower   *Estranged love*
Magnolia   *Love of nature*
Mallow, Syrian   *Consumed by love*
Marvel of Peru   *Flame of love*

Moss   *Maternal love*
Motherwort   *Concealed love*
Myrtle   *Love*
Narcissus   *Self-love*
Pink, Red, Double   *Pure and ardent love*
Pink, Single   *Pure love*
Rose   *Love*
Rose, Bridal   *Happy love*
Rose, Cabbage   *Ambassador of love*
Rose, Campion   *Only deserve my love*
Rose, Carolina   *Love is dangerous*
Rose, Maiden Blush   *If you love me you will find it out*
Rose, Yellow   *Decrease of love*
Scabious   *Unfortunate love*
Sweet Briar, Yellow   *Decrease of love*
Tuberose   *Voluptuous love*
Tulip, Red   *Declaration of love*
Tulip, Yellow   *Hopeless love*
Virgin's Bower   *Filial love*
Willow, Creeping   *Love forsaken*
Woodbine   *Fraternal love*

LOVE

VARIEGATED AND YELLOW TULIPS AND RED ROSEBUDS

The variegated tulips in this posy are a compliment to the recipient's 'beautiful eyes'; the red rosebuds say 'pure and lovely'; but the yellow hint at mystery or thwarted passion for their message is 'hopeless love.' In Victorian times, a lover might declare his passion by presenting a red rosebud just beginning to open. If this was accepted and worn, he could safely assume his attentions were welcome and follow up his first gift with a half-blown rose, and that with a full-blown one. If a Victorian woman wore the last, she was considered engaged. Cleopatra was well aware of the erotic symbolism of roses. She went to meet her lover Mark Antony in 42 BC in a room covered to a depth of two feet in roses. For the Romans it was the flower of beauty, love and poetry and dedicated to Venus, the goddess of love. In medieval times knights wore roses embroidered on their sleeves as a sign that gentleness should accompany courage and that beauty is the true reward of valour.

LOVE (DECLARATION OF LOVE)
TULIP — *Tulipa*

A favourite flower of the East, the name tulip derives from the Turkish word *tulband*, a turban, because of the shape of the flower. In Persia it is the emblem of consuming love and the means by which a young man declares his love and affection. He presents his mistress with a red tulip, which is meant to convey that his countenance is all on fire and his heart (symbolized by the black base) burnt to a coal. Tulips were said to be special to fairies and elves, who sang their babies to sleep beneath them and protected those who cultivated them. In Europe they quickly became firm favourites, especially in Holland where, between 1634-7 Tulipomania gripped the country. Bulbs were exchanged for enormous sums and a huge speculative market grew up which threatened to destabilize the country's economy. Many made their fortunes, but when the bubble eventually burst, yet more were ruined. Gerard and Parkinson recommended the roots preserved in sugar as a good and wholesome sweet with tonic properties.

LUXURY
or LUXURIANCE
HORSE CHESTNUT – *Aesculus hippocastanum*

"For in its honour prodigal nature weaves
A princely vestment, and profusely showers
O'er its green masses of broad palmy leaves,
Ten thousand waxen pyramidal flowers;
And gay and gracefully its head it heaves
Into the air, and monarch-like it towers."
WILLIAM HOWITT

Matthiolus (1501-77) wrote that the Turks called the fruits of this plant 'horse chestnuts' because they helped cure horses of a difficulty in breathing. The trees are very stately and grow to a great height, but the timber is too light to be of much value and the ripe seeds, known to British children as conkers, are edible only by sheep, cattle, horses and deer. The horse chestnut is made to represent luxury in the language of flowers because of the beauty of its foliage and the richness of its flowers.

MAJESTY AND POWER
IMPERIAL CROWN – *Fritillaris imperialis*

"The Crown Imperial; Lilies of all kinds,
The fleur-de-luce being one! O, these I lack,
To make you garlands of."
WILLIAM SHAKESPEARE

The very name of this flower speaks of majesty and power and certainly the crown-like and more than regal appearance of its hanging flowers and tuft of leaves above them supports the royal notion. It was introduced from Persia in the sixteenth century and George Chapman, writing in 1575, called it "Fayre Crowne-imperiall, Emperor of flowers". At the bottom of each flower bell there are drops of sweet water – Gerard says six drops in each flower. In German legend these "tears" are carried by the plant in sorrow and shame for not having bowed its head with the other plants on the night of Christ's agony.

MALEVOLENCE

LOBELIA – *Lobelia*

The reasons why this popular little bedding plant should have gained such a black reputation have been buried in the mists of time. They are a familiar and cheerful sight in window boxes and hanging baskets, although in equatorial Africa there are lobelias of giant proportions (up to twenty feet), from which may have originated a suggestion of menace. The lobelia was named by Linnaeus in honour of Matthias de Lobel, a remarkable man and a true founder of botanical science. Lobel was born at Lisle in 1538 and worked as a physician to William, Prince of Orange. He travelled a great deal and in his wanderings picked up an extensive knowledge of plants. He settled in England where, under the patronage of Lord Zouche, he established a physic garden at Hackney, east London and in due time was appointed King's Botanist by James I.

MARRIAGE
or FIDELITY IN FRIENDSHIP

IVY – *Hedera helix*

Ivy is not, as many suppose, a parasite; it roots extensively in the ground and does not need to penetrate deeply the surface to which it clings. It is a kindly plant, supportive in its clinging habit, providing nesting cover for birds without damaging the tree or wall up which it climbs. The way in which it protects and embraces has thus led to its meaning. In ancient Greece the altar of Hymen was encircled with ivy, and a branch of it was presented to a newly-wed couple as a symbol of their indissoluble knot. It represents love, constancy, dependence, fidelity and friendship and, like holly, is a symbol of immortality. A country girl would place a twig of ivy in her pocket and expect the next man she met to be her husband. Bacchus was crowned with a wreath of ivy and vine leaves. It was said that an alcoholic would be cured if he drank from a cup made of ivy wood. Ivy-berry vinegar was popular remedy in the Great Plague of 1665. Gold friendship brooches showing ivy growing round a fallen tree, with the motto "Nothing can detach me from it", were popular in Victorian times.

A MESSENGER

Iris – *Iris*

"Thou art the Iris, fair among the fairest,
Who, armed with golden rod
And winged with the celestial azure, bearest
The message of some God."

HENRY WADSWORTH LONGFELLOW

Iris was the daughter of Thaumas and Electra and a messenger of the gods, especially of Juno. As goddess of the rainbow, she is usually depicted descending from a glorious, colourful arch. The Greeks planted iris on tombs because the goddess was believed to guide the souls of dead women to their last resting place, as Mercury conducted the souls of men. Dedicated to Juno, iris was the symbol of eloquence or power and Egyptians placed the flower on the brow of the Sphinx and on the sceptres of their monarchs. The three petals of the flower are said to represent faith, wisdom and valour.

MIRTH

Crocus – *Crocus*

Dedicated to St Valentine, the crocus is one of the first spring flowers and welcomed by bees, who rush to them greedily – the furious sound they make as they brush up the pollen has been compared to "music made by a crowd of working people rendered half delirious by the discovery of a gold mine". They moved Homer to declare, "The flaming crocus made the mountain glow," and Greek myth tells of a beautiful youth, named Crocus, who was consumed by the ardency of his love for the shepherdess Smilax, and was afterwards metamorphosed into the flower. The Egyptians encircled their wine cups with garlands of crocus and saffron at banquets and the Greeks and Romans used it in their perfumes and essences. These were highly prized and made to flow in small streams at their entertainments, or descend in dewy showers over the audience. Gerard tells us that it was a drug which "maketh the sences more quicke and liuely, shaketh off heauie and drowsie sleepe, and maketh a man merrie".

MISTRUST

LAVENDER — *Lavandula officinalis*

"Lavender is for lovers true,
Which ever more be faine,
Desiring always for to have
Some pleasure for their paine."

The name lavender comes from *lavare*, to wash, and it was highly prized in ancient times for its refreshing perfume and cleansing properties. The Romans used it as a bath perfume to relieve fatigue and stiff joints. However, they always approached it with extreme caution, believing the plants to be a favourite haunt of the deadly asp, and they never used it in wreaths or garlands. For this reason it has become associated with the notion of mistrust. Lavender was highly respected, however, by herbalists who recommended it as a nerve stimulant and a reliever of aches, pains, sprains, rheumatism and flatulence. Powdered lavender was served as a condiment and Queen Elizabeth I much enjoyed conserve of lavender which, it was said, was always on her table. William Turner wrote in his *New Herball* (1551), "I judge that the flowers of Lavender quilted in a cap and worne are good for all diseases of the head that come from a cold cause and that they comfort the braine very well." It was placed between linen sheets to ward off moths and to scent them:

"In blanch'd linen, smooth and lavender'd."
JOHN KEATS

A sixteenth-century recipe for complexion water advises: "Take a gallon of faire water, one handfull of lauender floures and some few cloues and orace powder and foure ounces of Benjamin [a vegetable gum], distill the water in an ordinarie leaden still." In Spain and Portugal lavender is strewn on the floors of churches and houses on festive occasions.

"And Lavender, whose spikes of azure bloom
Shall be, erewhile, in arid bundles bound,
To lurk amidst the labours of her loom,
And crown her kerchiefs clean with mickle rare perfume."
WILLIAM SHENSTONE

MOURNING
or FORSAKEN LOVE
WEEPING WILLOW — *Salix babylonica*

"Thus o'er our streams do eastern willows lean
In pensive guise; whose grief-inspiring shade,
Love to melancholy sacred made."

JACQUES DELILLE

The willow is a funereal tree, planted along with yew and rosemary over graves, and emblematic of grief and loss. Spenser speaks of the "willow worn of forlorne paramours" and Shakespeare pictures Dido "a willow in her hand". The captive Children of Israel sat beneath willows as they wept and mourned "by the waters of Babylon". Medicinally, the white willow was used to right digestion and cure dysentery and chronic diarrhoea while the black was considered "an excellent remedy for all forms of eroticism, especially if the cause is due to local irritation." The willow wand is a favourite instrument of divination. So universal is its association with grief, sadness and loss that it came to be seen as an unlucky tree and even the poorest man hesitated to use it for firewood.

MUSIC
REED — *Phragmites communis*

Apollo was so offended when he heard that King Midas had expressed the opinion that Pan's reed-pipes produced better music than his lyre, that he changed the king's ears into those of an ass. Midas concealed his deformity as long as he could; but eventually a barber discovered his secret. Unable to keep it, but at the same time dreading the king's wrath, he dug a hole in the earth and whispered 'King Midas has the ears of an ass' into it before covering it up. On the spot, a number of reeds grew which, when agitated by the wind, were said not merely to rustle but to broadcast the buried words. Cato tells of Roman country people binding broken limbs with split reeds and uttering incantations over them. To dream of reeds indicates some brewing mischief between the dreamer and his friends.

NIGHT

Convolvulus – *Convolvulus*

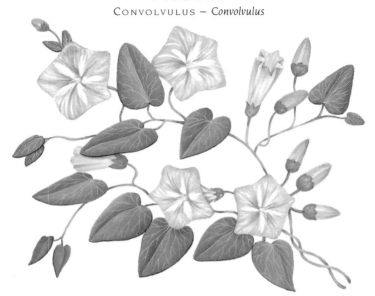

The association of convolvulus with the night – its flowers close up in the dark – comes through strongly in the local names given to it: nightcap (Wiltshire) and old man's nightcap (Sussex). However, its meaning may come from the convolvulus of the tropics, which only blooms at night. The lesser bindweed, *Convolvulus arvensis*, one of the most pernicious weeds, is known as devil's guts, or devil's garters in Ireland, because its roots penetrate the ground up to six feet. The *Convolvulus tricolour*, from Spain and Portugal, has many deep blue flowers which have yellow throats and white tubes. In the eighteenth century the species was known as the life of man, because, according to the Revd William Hanbury (A *Complete Book of Planting and Gardening*, 1770), "It has flower buds in the morning, which will be full blown by noon, and withered up before night." A purgative medicine called scammony is obtained from the root of *Convolvulus scammonia*, a perennial vine native to the Mediterranean.

ORACLE

D A N D E L I O N — *Leontodum taraxacum*

D andelion is a corruption of the French *dent de lion*, which in turn comes from the medieval apothecaries' term *dens leonis*, so-named because either the tap root, the florets, or the jagged edge of the leaves resemble a lion's tooth. It is also connected with the sun, as is the lion; the flower's appearance is very suggestive of ancient representations of the sun. It has many local names, including fairy clock, swine snout, priest's crown, puff ball and shepherd's clock and is known as the rustic oracle because its flowers always open at about 5 am and shut at 8 pm, serving the shepherd as a clock. In addition, the feathery seed-tufts serve as his barometer, predicting calm or storm. Children and lovers grant them special oracular powers and blow on them to judge the time, or to find out whether or not they are in their loved one's thoughts. They have long been used in salads and wine, are rich in vitamin A and are reputed to have curative and diuretic properties, hence the French name *pissenlit*.

ORNAMENT

HORNBEAM – *Carpinus betulus*

"Here hornbeam hedges regularly grow
Here hawthorn whitens and wild roses blow."

Hornbeam is also known as yoke elm, horse beech, horn elm and hard beam, because it grows so hard and tough with age that it is more like horn than wood. This hardness makes it suitable for agricultural implements and it was used by the Romans for yokes and beams for horned oxen. The leaves make good fodder for cattle and the bark a yellow dye, used in Sweden. It also makes excellent charcoal. French royal gardens were divided up by ornamental hedges of hornbeam, which keep their leaves in winter, hence the hornbeam became the symbol of ornament. In the country districts around Valenciennes, lovers still hang branches of hornbeam outside the door of their sweetheart's house on May Day morning as a symbol of their devotion. Medicinally, the leaves can be made into an infusion and drunk as a tonic and blood purifier.

PAINTING

AURICULA – *Primula auricula*

"Queen of the snowy alps, in glittering pride
She rears her palace on the mountain's side;
There, as bright sun-beams light her spangled throne."
GEORGE SHAW

Gerard called the auricula bear's-ear or mountain cowslip and tells us that the root was in great demand among Alpine hunters because of its reputed ability to strengthen the head and prevent giddiness and "swimming of the brain" overtaking them at high altitudes. The leaves were used as a styptic to heal wounds and old herbalists recommended it for palsy. It was highly regarded for its beauty and admired for the range of colours of its rich velvet corollas, some of which are the darkest purple, others a fine blue, bright yellow, delicate lilac, olive brown, pure white, variegated, bordered or mottled – exactly like a painter's palette.

PATERNAL ERROR

LADY'S SMOCK – *Cardamine pratensis*

"When Daisies pied, and Violets blue,
And Lady's Smocks all silver white,
And Cuckoo-buds of yellow hue,
Do paint the meadows with delight."
WILLIAM SHAKESPEARE

Lady's smock was made emblem of paternal error because it was one of the flowers which formed the garland crown of King Lear after he had made the mistake of relinquishing his royal crown to two of his scheming daughters. Another name, common in Shakepeare's time, was cuckoo-flower, from its "flowering for the most parte, in Aprille and Maie, when the Cuckowe doth begin to sing her pleasant notes without stammering". Lady's smock is one of the flowers dedicated to the Virgin Mary and was said by Prior to be so called because of the resemblance of its white flowers to little smocks hung out to dry. Other old names include milkmaids, pleasant-in-sight and spink.

PEACE

OLIVE – *Olea europæa*

The olive tree has a very ancient and romantic history. An olive branch has long been a universal symbol of peace. The dove returned to the ark bearing a fresh olive leaf, and was seen by Noah as the herald of peace and salvation. In China, a common method of making up a quarrel is to send the aggrieved person an olive and a piece of red paper, as a sign that peace is restored. For the Greeks, too, it was a token of peace and goodwill, carried to neighbours' houses at New Year. It is associated with Christ, the Prince of Peace, because it was on the Mount of Olives that he suffered, and it appears on the tombs of early martyrs. St Agnes is often depicted wearing a crown of olives and holding an olive branch. The oil is indispensable in cooking and has soothing medicinal properties. Delicate babies used to be massaged with olive oil and absorbed its nourishing properties well through their skin. To dream of olive trees bearing olives denotes peace, delight, concord, liberty, dignity and the fruition of your desires.

PENSIVENESS
Cowslip − *Primula veris*

"Cowslips wan that hang the pensive head."
JOHN MILTON

The familiar name cowslip derives from the Anglo-Saxon *cuslyppe*, or *cusloppe*, cowslime or cowpat, because the plant was supposed to spring up where cow-dung had fallen. The flowers of the common cowslip, pretty mullein, or paigle, are, in some parts of Kent, called fairy cups and Shakespeare refers to them in A *Midsummer Night's Dream*:

> *"In their gold coats spots, you see,*
> *Those be rubies, fairy favours,*
> *In those freckles live their savours."*

In Elizabethan times a delicious wine, said to resemble Muscatel and to induce deep sleep, was made from cowslips. Its meaning may arise from the mood of melancholy love poets often attributed to it.

PERFECT GOODNESS

Strawberry — *Fragaria*

The strawberry is the symbol of perfect righteousness, particularly of the righteous man whose fruits are good works. When displayed with other flowers and fruits, it represents not the righteous but rather their good works – the fruits of the spirit. It is therefore easy to understand why the Virgin Mary is sometimes shown clad in a dress decorated with clusters of strawberries. The strawberry is also occasionally shown accompanied by violets, suggesting that the truly spiritual are always humble and faithful. The strawberry's fruit, in particular, is made the symbol of perfect goodness because of its delicious flavour and fragrance:

> "The strawberry grows underneath the nettle;
> And wholesome berries thrive and ripen best,
> Neighbour's by fruit of baser quality."
> WILLIAM SHAKESPEARE

PERFECTION
PINEAPPLE – *Ananas*

Christopher Columbus found pineapples growing on the island of Guadeloupe in 1493 but they were not introduced to Britain until the seventeenth century. They were so-named because of their resemblance to extra-large cones from a pine tree, such cones having been formerly described as "pine-apples". They signify perfection because the ripe, juicy fruit tastes so delicious. Of all the exotic fruits grown by the British gardener of the eighteenth and nineteenth century, none excited more enthusiasm than the pineapple. The dining tables of great houses were considered incomplete without home-grown *ananas* displayed among the desserts. In June 1820, a Mr John Edwards of Glamorganshire presented King George IV with a pineapple which weighed nine pounds, four ounces, and, a year later, Lord Cawdor's gardener grew a fruit weighing ten pounds, eight ounces, which stood ten and a half inches high and was part of the dessert at the Coronation banquet.

PERPLEXITY
LOVE-IN-A-MIST – *Nigella diamascena*

The 'mist' is the involucre of finely divided bracts surrounding the flower, which prompted a host of country names, including fennel-flower, bishopswort, chase the devil, devil-in-a-bush, Jack in prison, Katherine's flower, Kiss-me-twice-before-I-rise, love entangle, love-in-a-puzzle, old man's beard, blackcumin and the French *cheveux de Venus*, which evidently had sexual hair in mind. The suggestiveness of many of these names implies the "perplexity" called love. The "devil" was the horned capsule at the centre of the flower surrounded by a bush of finely divided fringe, or "mist". Also known as flower of St Catherine, the flowers were said to represent the spokes of her wheel of martyrdom. In the East love-in-a-mist is used to flavour curries and bread and the French use the seeds which have a spicy, pungent taste, as a substitute for pepper and call them *quatre épices* or *toute épice*. Medicinally it is used for digestive complaints and intermittent fevers, while in India it is given after childbirth.

PITY

PINE — *Pinus*

"The loud wind through the forest wakes
With sounds like ocean roaring, wild and deep,
And in yon gloomy Pines strange music makes,
Like symphonies unearthly, heard in sleep;
The sobbing waters wash their waves and weep,
Where moans the blast its dreary path along,
The bending Firs a mournful cadence keep."

WILLIAM DRUMMOND

The pine has an ancient and incident-packed history. A number of people have been metamorphosed into a pine tree, including Atys after he had broken his vow of celibacy to Cybele, the mother of the gods. She mourned his loss beneath the branches until Jupiter, out of pity, promised that the pine should remain evergreen. It is dedicated to Bacchus and also to Pan, because Pitys, one of the many nymphs Pan loved, was changed into a pine tree to escape the embraces of Boreas. It is also dedicated to Neptune, the god of the sea, because pine wood was used in the construction of the first ships. Turnus set fire to the Trojan fleet with a flaming brand of pine (kept alight by the resin of the cones). An unopened pine cone symbolized virginity. A Roman myth tells of two lovers who died, were buried in the same cemetery and changed into a pine and a vine so that they could continue their fond embraces. Ovid crowned the fauns with pine and Virgil called it *Pronuba* because the torches used at weddings were made of pine wood. In Japan the pine has become a symbol of constancy and conjugal fidelity because it is always verdant, even beneath the snow. Its evergreen foliage led to it becoming a symbol of immortality and generation and, like the cypress and the fir, its branches were often placed on coffins. Traditionally, it is said to have been one of the trees from which Christ's cross was made and the Christmas tradition of erecting a small pine tree in the house full of candles, fruit and special decorations with gaily wrapped presents placed beneath survives today.

"Yon verdant pines, that midst the winter smile,
Offspring of Scotia or Virginia's soil."

JACQUES DELILLE

125

YOU PLEASE ALL

BRANCH OF CURRANTS — *Ribes*

"They butter'd currants on fat veal bestow'd,
And rumps of beef with virgin honey stew'd."

Currants were popularly called "berries of St John" because they begin to ripen around St John's Day, 24 June. Lyte, writing in 1578, calls redcurrants "Bastard Corinthes". The Victorians cherished their soft fruits, making them into pies, summer puddings, jams, jellies and wines, and therefore selected currants to represent the motto "You please all". Arthur Young, a nineteenth-century agriculturist, supplies a recipe for what he calls "Family Wine", which, he maintains, is guaranteed to put a surplus of blackcurrants, redcurrants, white currants, ripe cherries and raspberries, to good use. The thick juice of blackcurrants simmered with sugar formed a popular nightcap in medieval times. It was also taken for sore throats and quinsy (tonsilitis), hence its country names quinsyberry and squinancy berries.

POETRY

SWEET BRIAR OR EGLANTINE – *Rosa Rubiginosa* or *Eglanteria*

The sweet briar is generally understood to be the eglantine of old English poets. Chaucer spelt the word "eglatere"

> *"The hegge also, that yede in compas,*
> *And closed in all the greene herbere,*
> *With Sicamour was set and Eglatere."*

It figures in the poetry of Shakespeare, Spenser, Shenstone, Walter Scott, Keats, and Milton. Judas Iscariot was said to have hanged himself on the eglantine and the devil was supposed to have used the thorns as a ladder to try to reascend to heaven. But he was thwarted by God, who would not permit the eglantine to grow upwards, but only to extend itself as a bush. Out of spite, the devil then turned the thorns downwards pointing towards the earth.

POPULAR FAVOUR

ROCK ROSE – *Cistus*

"From fairest creatures we desire increase
That thereby beauty's Rose might never die."
WILLIAM SHAKESPEARE

To the Victorians "popular" meant "superficial" in this sense and the cistus or rock rose was made emblem of popular favour because it has a beautiful, though frail and transient flower. The blooms last only a few hours, dropping off soon after noon, but a plentiful supply of buds ensures the procession of colour lasts for some weeks each summer. On Greek islands oil from the foliage, wiped off and collected with a leather-thonged rake, is made into a crude form of incense known as ladanum. (Ladanum is thought to have been the Myrrh of the Bible.) Herodotus described another method of collection: "Ladanum is found in a most incongruous place. It is the sweetest of scented substances. It is gathered from the beards of he-goats, where it is found sticking, like gum, having come from the bushes on which they browse."

PRAISE (WORTHY OF PRAISE)

FENNEL – *Fœniculum vulgare*

In ancient Greece garlands of fennel were presented to victorious warriors, and it was believed to bestow strength, courage and long life. Medicinally it was used to treat kidney complaints, stings, bites and ague; and the whole plant – root, stem, leaf and seeds – was taken for lung infections, ear troubles and eyesight problems. Pliny recorded that serpents sharpened their sight with the juice by rubbing against the plant and the belief persisted for some time that it helped to clear vision. The green leaves were given to nursing mothers to ensure an abundance of milk and it is still included in infants' gripe water. It was a common practice among the hungry poor to eat fennel to reduce hunger pains and it has been used for centuries as a slimming aid. Fennel was thought to have benevolent powers and to thwart witchcraft. Bedchambers were protected from malignant spirits by stuffing the keyholes with fennel.

PRECAUTION

GOLDEN ROD — *Solidago virgaurea*

Golden rod was formerly called wound-weed because of its healing powers. In Elizabethan times it was brought from abroad in a dried state and sold in London markets by herb-women for as much as half-a-crown an ounce. However, when it was discovered growing in Hampstead ponds, its value crashed, which, wrote Gerard "plainely setteth forth our inconstancie and sudden mutabilitie, esteeming no longer of anything, how pretious soever it be, than whilest it is strange and rare. This verifieth our English proverbe, 'Far fetch and deare bought is best for ladies.'" Traditionally, golden rod was used as a divining rod to find not just hidden springs of water, but also treasures of gold and silver. Also known as goldruthe, solidago and Aaron's rod, a yellow dye was once made from the leaves and flowers. Astrologers say that golden rod is a plant of Venus.

PRECOCITY

MAY ROSE — *Rosa cinnamoma*

"Oh! sooner shall the rose of May
Mistake her own sweet nightingale,
And to some meaner minstrel's lay
Open her bosom's glowing veil,
Than Love shall ever doubt a tone,
A breath of the beloved one."
THOMAS MOORE

This early, aromatic rose was made to represent precocity because it is one of the first roses to bloom. According to Moslem legend, the first rose sprang from the beads of sweat of the prophet Mohammed; in Persia, the flower was a symbol of beauty, virtue, poetry, women and love.

"She must no more a-Maying,
Or by Rosebuds divine
Who'll be her Valentine."
ROBERT HERRICK

PREFERENCE
APPLE BLOSSOM – *Malus sylvestris*

"What if you have seen it before, ten thousand times over? An apple-tree in full blossom is like a message, sent fresh from heaven to earth, of purity and beauty!"

HENRY WARD BEECHER

The delight an apple tree in blossom evokes in us, and the anticipation we have of the delicious fruits to come, has secured for it the emblem of preference. To dream of apples betokens long life, success in trade, or a lover's faithfulness. However, in Northamptonshire and also in the west of England, the blooming of the apple tree after the fruit is ripe is regarded as a sure omen of death:

"A bloom on the tree when the Apples are ripe
Is a sure termination to somebody's life."

It has been adopted as the state flower of Arkansas and Michigan.

PRESUMPTION

SNAPDRAGON — *Antirrhinum majus*

"The stern and furious lion's gaping mouth."
JUNIUS MODERATUS COLUMELLA

The snapdragon is presumptious in two ways: unless carefully cultivated, it will take over, springing up where gardeners' least expect
or want it; and its jaw-like flowers assume the look of an animal. It is
also known as lion's snap, toad's mouth, dog's mouth and calf's snout.
It was believed by country people to possess supernatural powers and
was worn as a protection from witchcraft.

> *"There used to be much snapdragon growing on the walls opposite
> my freshman's rooms there (Trinity College), and I had for years
> taken it as the emblem of my own perpetual residence, even unto
> death, in my university."*
>
> CARDINAL NEWMAN

PRIDE

AMARYLLIS – *Amaryllis*

The dazzling splendour of the amaryllis in full bloom has often been compared to a haughty, beautiful woman, in her prime and fashionably dressed, who eclipses the quiet attractions of those around her, although their beauty is often destined to outlast that of their proud and disdainful rival.

"When Amaryllis fair doth show, the richness of her fiery glow,
The modest lily hides her head; the former seems so proudly spread
To win the gaze of human eye, which soonest brightest things doth spy.
Yet vainly is the honour won, since hastily her course is run;
She blossoms, blooms – she fades, she dies – they who admired, now despise."

A humbling lesson to the young and vain. The word amaryllis signifies splendour in the Greek language.

PROFIT

CABBAGE – *Brassica*

"That herb, which o'er the whole terrestrial globe
Doth flourish, and in great abundance yields
To low plebeian, and the haughty king,
In winter, cabbage; and green sprouts in spring."
JUNIUS MODERATUS COLUMELLA

Cabbage is a very proper emblem of profit as there are many garden kinds of great value and they have long played a beneficial role as both food and medicine. Monks cultivated them in their gardens, as physical labour was regarded as an exercise that defined the spirit, and St Jerome urged young monks to "hoe your ground, set out cabages, convey water to them in conduits". In ancient Greece cabbages were said to have sprung from the tears of Lycurgus. Romans believed the vegetable kept them in good health and, optimistically, that it acted as an aphrodisiac. It was said to be good for failing sight, coughs and breathlessness.

PROHIBITION
or DEFENCE
PRIVET – *Ligustrum*

The name may derive from the same linguistic root as "private", but it is more likely that the real origin of the word has been lost. It was known as privet, from the Old English pryfet, as early as 1548, and was used extensively to enclose gardens and ensure privacy. It has a number of local names, some of which, like black tops and blue poison, refer to its berries. In Cornwall it has become known as skedge, skidgery and skedgewith, names which come from Cornish words for "shade tree". The liquid in which the leaves had been boiled was recommended for curing mouth and throat infections, although the fruits – small, black, shiny berries – are poisonous to man. At one time the fruits of the wild privet were collected and a crimson dye extracted. This was added to alum to form a deep green colour.

PROTECTION
JUNIPER – *Juniperus*

"Sweet is the Juniper, but sharp is his bough."
EDMUND SPENSER

Birds, insects and small woodland creatures seek the protection afforded by juniper, which, with its long branches and strong scent, conceals them from pursuers and predators. In Italy juniper is regarded with great veneration because, the story goes, it saved the life of Mary and the infant Jesus when they fled into Egypt. In order to screen her son from the assassins employed by Herod to put young children to death, Mary is said to have hidden him under a juniper tree. Because of this the juniper has been invested with the power of putting to flight the spirits of evil, hence sprigs of juniper are hung outside stables and houses to preserve them from the power of witches. In Germany, when a child fell ill, the parents hid a bunch of juniper in some bread and wool, in order to induce bad spirits to eat, to spin and so forget the poor suffering child. The berries are used for the production of Geneva or Dutch gin, and in Sweden a healthy beer is made from them.

PROVIDENCE

CLOVER (PURPLE) – *Trifolium pratense*

"If you find an even Ash-leaf or a four-leaved Clover,
You'll be bound to see your true lover ere the day be over."

The triple leaf of the clover, or trefoil, to use its old English name, has been associated with the Holy Trinity since St Patrick used it to illustrate the doctrine of the Three in One. Clover is used for decorations on Trinity Sunday and is often employed as an architectural emblem: the limbs of crosses are sometimes made to end in trefoils, and church windows are frequently in the same form. Hope was depicted by the ancients as a little child standing on tiptoe, holding a clover-flower in his hand. Summer is also represented with the trefoil. Apart from bringing good luck, a four-leaved clover reputedly gave second sight and the power to detect witches and see fairies. To dream of a field of clover indicates health, prosperity and much happiness. To the lover it foretells success, and that his intended wife will be wealthy.

PRUDENCE

MOUNTAIN ASH OR ROWAN – *Sorbus aucuparia*

*"If your whip-stick's made of Row'n,
You may ride your nag through any town."*

The mountain ash, or rowan tree, is also known as rodden, quicken-tree and witchen-tree, and is a tree of good omen. It used to be thought prudent to carry small crosses made of its wood, or to hang sprays of its leaves from rafters, for protection from witches and to prevent any evil spirits entering the house or cattle shed. In Scandinavian mythology it is called Thor's helper, because it bent to his grasp when he was crossing the river Vimur on his way to the land of the Frost Giants. Norse ships were built from rowan wood to preserve them from Ran, who delighted in drowning sailors. The rowan is associated both with Druids, for whom it was said to be held sacred, and with pixies, who were said to use it as a trysting place. These connections explain why so many superstitions surround it.

PURITY

WHITE LILY — *Lilium candidum* and STAR OF BETHLEHEM —
Ornithogalum umbellatum

"Ye loftier lilies, bath'd in morning dew,
Of purity and innocence renew
Each lovely thought."
BERNARD BARTON

A ccording to an ancient Christian legend, the first lily "sprang from the tears of Eve as she went from Eden". However, long before Christianity, the white lily was held in the highest regard by the Greeks and Romans, and was one of the flowers incorporated into the couch of Juno and Jupiter. There is a story that the flower sprang up where drops of Juno's celestial milk fell as the infant Hercules was greedily suckling at her breast. The white lily is the emblem of purity and dedicated to the Virgin Mary. When doubting Thomas insisted her tomb be opened to see if she had, indeed, been resurrected, he found it was filled only with beautiful roses and white lilies. The flower comes into bloom about the time of the Annunciation and is always used to decorate the altar of the Virgin Mary. The crucifix twined with the Madonna lily signifies devotion and purity of heart.

"Lilies are by plain direction
Emblems of a double kind;
Emblems of thy fair complexion,
Emblems of thy fairer mind."
NATHANIEL COTTON

T he Star of Bethlehem is so-called from the supposed resemblance of the pure white, star-shaped flower to the star which illuminated the sky immediately above the birthplace of Jesus Christ. Jesus said "Consider the Lilies how they grow; they toil not, they spin not: and yet I say unto you, that even Solomon in all his glory was not arrayed like one of these." It was also known as eleven o'clock lady, because it does not open its petals much before eleven; Jack-go-to-bed-at-noon, Dove's dung and bird's milk.

"While the Lily white shall in love delight,
Nor a thorn nor a threat stain her beauty bright."
WILLIAM BLAKE

QUICK-SIGHTEDNESS

HAWKWEED – *Heiracium*

Hawkweed or hawk-bit acquired its name because, says Pliny, "hawks tear it apart and wet their eyes with the juice, so dispelling dimness of sight, when it comes on them". That hawks fed upon the plant and encouraged their young ones to do so in order to sharpen their eyesight was a popular belief throughout Europe, where falconry was an important sport. Gerard also wrote that hawks were reported to clear their sight by "conveying the juice hereof into their eyes". Hawks were sacred birds to the Greeks and so hawkweed was considered a holy plant. *Heiracium aurantiacum* was also known as Grim the collier, because of the black hairs which cover its stem and involucre. Hawkweed was considered good for strengthening human eyesight, too; it was also deemed efficacious against the bites of serpents and scorpions. Culpeper recommend "a scruple of the dried root given in wine and vinegar is profitable for dropsy. The decoction of one herb taken in honey digesteth the phlegm in the chest or lungs, and with hyssop helps the cough."

RECONCILIATION

FILBERT OR HAZELNUT – *Corylus*

A good crop of hazelnuts was said to foretell disasters: "Many nuts, Many pits", ran the old saying (the pits referring to graves). However, a heavy crop of nuts could also signify plenty of babies. In addition, it was believed that if a double hazelnut was carried around in the pocket, the person would never suffer from toothache. On Hallowe'en, it was the custom for young girls to place a row of hazelnuts on the hot embers of a fire. Each girl in turn would then utter the name of her favourite man, and if the nut jumped, the match would be a successful one: "If you love me, pop and fly/If not, lie and die." The hazel features in early folklore. In Celtic times the tree was associated with both fertility and fire. Small hazel twigs kept in the house were supposed to protect it from lightning; kept on a boat they would preserve it from shipwreck. It was also used by water diviners who cut their rods from hazel trees after sunset, but before sunrise, taking care to face east to catch the first rays of the sun.

REFUSAL

CARNATION OR STRIPED PINK – *Dianthus*

"Bring Coronations, and Sops in wine,
Worn of paramours."
EDMUND SPENSER

Carnations, called Incarnacyon by William Turner in 1538, have strong religious associations – they were known as the divine flower, God made flesh, the Passion, drops of Christ's blood, as well as gillyflower, July-flower, coronations and sops in wine. Marie Antoinette, while imprisoned in Paris in 1793, was said to have been sent an escape plan written on a slip of paper concealed inside the calyx of a carnation. Unknown to her, however, the note had been intercepted, and although she was allowed to reply to it, agreeing to the proposed escape (she pricked out her message of assent on a scrap of paper with a needle), her answer never reached her friends and she went to the guillotine two months later.

RELIGIOUS SUPERSTITION

PASSION FLOWER – *Passiflora incarnata*

The passion flower was of great significance throughout Christendom. It was so named by Jesuit priests in the sixteenth century, who followed the victorious conquistadors through South America, seeking to convert the Indians to Christianity. Inspired by strong religious zeal, they imagined they could detect in this plant both the sequence of Christ's Passion and divine approval for their mission. It was called the flower of the five wounds because the five stamens were seen as symbolizing Christ's five wounds: the three parted stigma, the nails; one for each of the hands; the other for the feet, and the ovary, the hammer with which the wounds were made. The ten sepals and petals of its bloom represented the ten faithful Apostles (Judas and doubting Thomas – Peter in some versions – being excluded); the inner corona was thought to be the crown of thorns and the curling tendrils were supposed to be a reminder of the whips with which the Saviour was scourged.

REMEMBRANCE

ROSEMARY – *Rosmarinus officinalis*

"There's Rosemary, that's for remembrance."
WILLIAM SHAKESPEARE

Sir Thomas More wrote: "As for Rosmarine. I lett it runne all over my garden walls, not onlie because my bees love it, but because it is the herb sacred to remembrance, and, therefore, to friendship; whence a sprig of it hath a dumb language that maketh it the chosen emblem of our funeral wakes and in our buriall grounds." In Christian culture it is among the holiest of flowers, associated with the Virgin Mary and with Christ (it is said that it will never grow taller than Christ as He appeared on earth), and is seen as a defence against evil. Arab herbalists used it to restore strength, memory and speech and the Elizabethans to cure headaches, brain disorders and toothache. It was also used as a hair-restorer and its ashes for tooth powder to counteract blackened teeth. It was included in bunches of aromatic herbs taken into court during a trial as a protection against jail-fever and was burnt in sickrooms and hospitals.

REMORSE

RASPBERRY – *Rubus*

Remorse is represented by the thorny raspberry whose cruel prickles can cling to clothing and lacerate the flesh. In New Zealand these prickly *Rubus* are known to colonists as Bush Lawyers – because it is much easier to get into their clutches than out of them! Raspberries have long been a part of our diet. Palaeobotanists working on prehistoric settlements in Switzerland have discovered that the inhabitants' diet included raspberries, cherries, sloes and hazelnuts. Henry VIII was fond of raspberries and had his kitchen gardeners grow them at Hampton Court. In some counties of England they are known as hindberries. To dream of raspberries signifies success, happiness in marriage, fidelity in a sweetheart or good news from abroad. Raspberry leaf tea was used as a gargle for sore mouths and as a wash for wounds and ulcers.

RESERVE

Maple − *Acer campestre*

"On sods of turf he sat, the soldiers round;
A maple throne, rais'd higher from the ground,
Receiv'd the Trojan chief."

Ænis

The maple was made emblem of reserve because its flowers are late in opening and slow to fall. The wood of the maple was considered by Pliny to be the most elegant and firm and it was much in demand for inordinately expensive tables for Roman nobles. When these men accused their wives of extravagance, the woman literally "turned the tables" on their husbands. Pliny also recommended the pounded root as a remedy for pains in the liver. Medieval drinking vessels, known as mazers, were made from maple wood. In some parts of England it was believed that long life could be ensured for children if they were passed between the branches of a maple tree.

RESISTANCE

Tansy − *Tanacetum vulgare*

"Before my door the box-edg'd border lies,
Where flowers of mint, and thyme, and tansy rise."

Walter Scott

Tansy came to signify resistance because it was supposed to prevent the spread of contagious diseases. Its name derives from the Greek *athanasia*, meaning immortality, and both the ancient Greeks and Romans used it to preserve dead bodies from decay. Elizabethans employed it to treat internal wounds, and Culpeper declared it to be a herb that will help women conceive and "is their best companion, the husband excepted". A Sussex charm against ague consisted of wearing tansy leaves in the shoe. In the fifteenth and sixteenth centuries tansy was also a familiar part of daily diets. Both the leaves and the flowers of the plant were used, fresh or dried, and tansy puddings, custards, wine and tea were popular. Tansy cake was a favourite Easter dish, believed to purify the bodily system after the meagre fare of Lent.

RETALIATION

SCOTCH THISTLE — *Onopordium acanthium*

*"Proud Thistle, emblem dear to Scotland's sons,
Begirt with threatening points, strong in defence,
Unwilling to assault."*

Tradition has it that the Scotch thistle was originally planted on the rocky cliffs near Dumbarton Castle by Mary, Queen of Scots. It is the emblem of Scotland and is said to have been adopted because it saved the ancient Scots from a party of invading Norsemen: while attempting to attack under the cover of darkness, one of the invaders trod upon a prickly thistle and his cry of pain roused the Scots, who flew to arms and chased the foe from the field. It therefore came to betoken resistance and retaliation and is coupled with the motto *Nemo me impune lacessit* (rendered in homely Scottish as "Wha daur meddle wi' me" – or "No one shall provoke me with impunity"). To dream of being surrounded by thistles is a lucky omen, portending joyous news.

RETURN OF HAPPINESS

Lily-of-the-Valley — *Convallaria majalis*

"And sweetest to the view,
The Lily of the vale, whose virgin flower
Trembles at every breeze beneath its leafy bower."

The lily-of-the-valley, which announces the happy season of May, was dedicated to Ostara, the Norse goddess of Springtime and later, in Christian times, to the Virgin Mary. It was known as ladder-to-heaven and virgin's tears and is considered a symbol of humility and chastity because of its whiteness and the fact that the flower bows its head as if in mourning. The flowers, distilled in wine and stored in gold or silver vessels, were, in Gerard's time, "counted more precious than gold". An old English folktale relates the story of a three-day battle fought between St Leonard and a ferocious dragon named Sin. The saint finally won but was grieviously injured and it was said that wherever his blood dripped to the earth, there grew a lily-of-the-valley.

RICHES

"Now came the fulfilment of the year's desire
The tall wheat coloured by the August fire."
WILLIAM MORRIS

Nutritious golden wheat, the staff of life, is an appropriate emblem of riches. Wheat is the oldest of all the cereals cultivated by man and was known in the Stone Age, the Neolithic Age and in the Ancient World, where it was worshipped as a god. The Hittites had a harvest goddess called Ibritz; the Egyptians, Nepri; the Greeks, Demeter, and the Romans, Ceres, daughter of the god Saturn. Ceres' hair was the colour of corn and she is generally represented as a beautiful woman with a garland of ears of corn on her head, a wheatsheaf by her side and the cornucopia, or horn of plenty, in her hand. In India wheat is regarded as the emblem of fertility and two handfuls of corn are scattered over the clasped hands of the bride and bridegroom at weddings. The Chinese regard corn as a gift from heaven and celebrate with prayers, sacrifices and religious rites, both at seed time and harvest. According to tradition, Adam took three things with him when driven out of Paradise – an ear of corn, chief of all kinds of food; a bunch of dates, chief of fruits; and a slip of myrtle, chief of sweet-scented flowers. In England the corn dolly, a potent symbol of regeneration and riches, was plaited by the oldest farm worker from the last stook of corn as it stood in the harvest field. With great ceremony, it was then taken into the farmhouse, where it hung over the hearth until the following harvest, when it was replaced by a dolly from the new crop. The corn dolly, or kern baby, was believed to bring good fortune – an idea that survives today in the church Harvest Festival, during which the font is decorated with wheat, fruit and flowers. The same reverence for corn extended to bread itself. Regarded as the embodiment of the corn spirit, it was considered unlucky to throw bread away, and even more so to burn it. Bread baked on Christmas Day was expected to protect the home against sickness.

"For the few hours of life allotted me
Give me Great God but Bread and Libertie."
ABRAHAM COWLEY

RIVALRY

Rocket — *Hesperis matronalis*

Rocket is said to have first appeared in London in the spring succeeding the Great Fire of 1666. Young plants were seen everywhere, springing up among the ruins in such profusion that by the summer, people were astonished by the enormous crop. It originated in the Mediterranean and is sometimes known as Italian cress. Pliny claimed, "Whosoever taketh the seed of Rocket before he be whipt, shall be so hardened that he shall easily endure the paines." It has also been linked with falsehood and deceit because it appears to possess no fragrance by day, but under cover of night gives off a strong scent. Turner recommended the seeds "against the bitings of the shrew-mouse and other venomous beasts", and also believed them to have aphrodisiac properties. Mixed with vinegar and honey, the seeds were used as a beauty preparation to remove freckles and pimples. The double white rocket was said to have been Marie Antoinette's favourite flower and so was known as fair maid of France.

SAFETY

Traveller's Joy — *Clematis vitalba*

John Gerard, writing in 1597, referred to this rampant climber "decking and adorning waies and hedges, where people travell, and thereupon I have named it Traveller's Ioie". He also called it virgin's bower because it could form a suitable arbour in which young girls could sit, protected from the summer sunshine and passers-by – hence it came to represent safety and rest. It has white flowers succeeded by round, white and silky seedheads which persist for months and have inspired many country names: old man's beard, old man's woozard, grandfather's whiskers, snow in the harvest and hedge feathers. Other names, like burning bush, smoking cane, tobacco and boys' bacca, stem from an old country practice: small boys used to smoke cigar lengths of the stems, as they are hollow and do not burn easily. A preparation made from the bruised roots and stems of *clematis vitalba*, boiled and then placed in sweet oil, was formerly used as a cure for itching. It was taken internally in the form of a powder to cure pains in the bones.

SATIRE

PRICKLY PEAR — *Opuntia ficus-indica*

"Satire should, like a polished razor keen,
Wound with a touch that's scarcely felt or seen."
LADY MARY WORTLEY MONTAGU

The prickly pear is a cactus. It produces fruits of excellent quality, called Indian figs, which are reputed to be highly nutritious – they can be eaten fresh or dried and cooked in various ways. Other by-products of *Opuntias* include fruit syrups, a paste made by boiling down the juice, and a fermented drink called coloncha. In spring the tender young shoots, flowers and bulbs are eaten as vegetables and the leaves used as poultices to relieve inflammation. The juice is also employed in the manufacture of candles; gum is extracted from the stem and the plants are fed to stock after the spines have been burnt off with torches. In spite of all these good qualities, the prickly pear has become a troublesome weed in Australia, South Africa and India.

SENSITIVITY

MIMOSA – *Mimosa*

A native of Brazil, the *Mimosa pudica* is known as the "sensitive plant" because of its touch-sensitive foliage. The leaves collapse beneath the feet when walked upon, but after a while they expand to their normal size. In Indian mythology the mimosa was the tree said to have sprung from the claw lost by a falcon when it tried to steal the heavenly Soma, or Amrita, the drink of immortality, for the gods who were pining for it. The attempt was successful but the falcon was wounded by an arrow fired by one of the demons guarding the precious beverage and lost a claw and a feather, which fell to earth and struck root. The claw became the Indian thorn-tree or *Mimosa catechu*, which has the ability to withdraw its leaves if touched. A sprig worn in the turban, or suspended over the bed, was thought to be a preservative against magic spells. The frankincense of the bible is the product of the Egyptian mimosa, a tree spoken of by Theophrastus as an Acanthus, and referred to by Virgil.

SHAME

P E O N Y — *Pæonia*

Peonies were among the earliest known medicinal plants, and they were named after Pæon, legendary physician to the gods of ancient Greece. Pliny wrote: "The most anciently discovered herb is the Peony, which still keeps its discoverer's name." People once believed that, apart from their remarkable curative properties, peonies had the power to keep away evil spirits and storms. They were also said to bestow long life. Necklaces of seeds were worn to counter shameful diseases like leprosy, lunacy, epilepsy and chronic nightmares, and the roots were also worn by children to help them cut their teeth. But digging them up was a highly dangerous undertaking, like digging up mandrakes. Peonies were said to shriek so horribly as they were uprooted that anyone nearby would die. The safest way to gather them was therefore thought to be to tie a dog to the plant and let the animal pull it up.

SHARPNESS OF TEMPER
or SOURNESS

B A R B E R R Y — *Barberis vulgaris*

"Conserve of Barbarie: quincies as such,
With sirops that easeth the sickly so much."
G O O D   H O U S E W I F E   P H Y S I C K E — 1573

The common barberry was considered one of the best of all liver tonics because its bitter principle was thought to be more closely allied to human bile than any other substance. It was used against jaundice, gall complaints and catarrh, and was thought to be a good remedy for diabetes because it allayed the thirst that often accompanies the disease. The barberry was formerly called the pipperidge bush, and was regarded with superstitious dislike by farmers, who believed that it injured wheat crops. The fruit of the barberry is so sharply acid that birds shun it and the flowers have a touch-me-not irritability, the stamens coiling around the pistil at the slightest touch. It is this trait that gives rise to the symbolism of bad temper.

SICKNESS

Wood Anemone – *Anemone nemorosa*

"So sudden fades the sweet Anemone.
The feeble stems, to stormy blasts a prey,
Their sickly beauties droop and pine away.
The wind forbids the flow'rs to flourish long,
Which owe to winds their name in Grecian song."

In classical mythology Anemone was a nymph beloved by the west wind, the gentle Zephyr, who was said to produce flowers and fruits by the sweetness of his breath. To shield her from the jealousy of Flora, he transformed her into this flower "most delicate", which he loved to caress. The name derives from the Greek *anemos* the wind, and the anemone is known as wind-flower in England and *Winderöschen*, little wind-rose, in Germany. It is traditionally a fairy flower and to fairy fingers is attributed the delicate pink pencilling with which the petals are frequently tinged. They are said "to nestle cosily inside the tent of leaves and draw the curtains close around" when night falls. The Egyptians first made the anemone emblem of sickness and Christian symbolism also associated it with illness. The anemone is depicted in scenes of Christ's death and also accompanying the Virgin Mary to show her sorrow for the Passion of Christ, for it is said that anemones sprang up on Calvary on the evening of the Crucifixion. It has a contradictory reputation for provoking and curing sickness. Some believed the air to be so tainted wherever wood anemones grew that simply to breathe it would cause severe sickness, while others recommended picking the first anemone of the season as a remedy against disease:

"The first spring-blown anemone she in his doublet wove,
To keep him safe from pestilence, wherever he should rove."

The flower's link with sorrow and death dates back to the legend of Adonis, the favourite of Venus, who was killed by a wild boar. Venus, to whom the flower is sacred, wept tears which turned into anemones:

"For while what's mortal from his blood she freed,
And showers of tears on the pale body shed,
Lovely Anemones in order rose,
And veiled with purple palls the cause of all her woes."
René Rapin

SILENCE

W A T E R L I L Y O R L O T U S F L O W E R – *Nymphaea lotus*

"*Now folds the lily all her sweetness up*
And slips into the bosom of the lake.
So fold thyself, my dearest, thou and slip
Into my bosom and be lost in me."
ALFRED TENNYSON

The water lily is symbolic of silence and of chastity. Its name derives from Lotis, Neptune's beautiful daughter, who was transformed into a lotus tree by the gods to keep her safe from the obscene caresses of Priapus. In German folklore, too, the belief persisted that water nymphs disguised themselves as water liles when harried by lustful males. The white rose also symbolizes silence. In classical times a single white rose used to be suspended over the guest table to signify that the diners could speak in complete confidence. The principle is with us today in white plaster ceiling roses.

SINCERITY

FERN – *Filicinae*

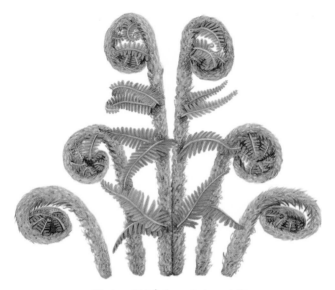

"But on St John's mysterious night,
Sacred to many a wizard spell,
The hour when first to human sight
Confest, the mystic Fern-seed fell."

Among Celtic and Germanic nations the fern was formerly considered a sacred and auspicious plant with the power to bring good luck and confer wealth; it was also purported that the bearer of a fern seed could be rendered invisible. In order for this wonder-working seed to have effect, however, it had to be caught at midnight on Midsummer's Eve by a bare-footed person in "a religious state of mind" The fern, with its watery associations, is dedicated to St Christopher and often referred to as St Christopher's herb. The root of the male fern was an important ingredient in old love potions. Culpepper recommended Royal Fern for "both inward and outward griefs."

SLEEP OF THE HEART

WHITE POPPY – *Papaver somniferumis*

> *"From the Poppy I have ta'en*
> *Mortal's balm, and mortal's bane!*
> *Juice, that creeping through the heart,*
> *Deadens ev'ry sense of smart;*
> *Doom'd to heal, or doom'd to kill,*
> *Fraught with good, or fraught with ill."*
> MRS M. ROBINSON

The white opium poppy was grown in ancient Egypt. Virgil speaks of the flower as "sleep bringing", and Morpheus, the Roman god of dreams, fashioned crowns of poppies to give to those he wanted to send to sleep. Spenser, too, describes it as the "dead, sleeping poppy". Around 1822, when De Quincey's *Confessions of an English Opium Eater* was published, opium was extensively grown in England and 50,000lb were consumed in one year as laudanum and morphine.

SOLITUDE

HEATH OR LICHEN – *Erica*

Solitude can most certainly be found on the wide open heathlands and heather-covered moors. Wordsworth wrote:

> *"And on these barren rocks, with juniper,*
> *And heath, and thistle, thinly sprinkled o'er,*
> *Fixing his downcast eye, he many an hour*
> *A morbid pleasure nourished, tracing here*
> *An emblem of his own unfruitful life."*

In the Hebrides a beer is made from heath, using two parts of the young tops to one part of malt and the ancient Picts were said by Boethius to have made a similar beer from heather flowers. There is a legend that, after the slaughter by Kenneth McAlpin, an early King of the Scots, the only surviving Picts, a father and son, were brought before the conqueror and offered their lives in exchange for the secret recipe – but they preferred to die than reveal it.

SORROW

Y EW — *Taxus baccata*

"The Yew, which, in the place of sculptured stone,
Marks out the resting-place of men unknown."

CHARLES CHURCHILL

As an evergreen, the yew was regarded as a symbol of immortality by the Greeks and Romans, who used it to fuel funeral pyres. For the ancient Egyptians it was a symbol of mourning; it was also sacred to the Druids. Its gloomy and sombre presence in churchyards and cemeteries never fails to conjure sorrow and sadness.

"Well do I know thee by thy trusty Yew,
Cheerless, unsocial plant, that loves to dwell
'Midst skulls and coffins, epitaphs, and worms;
Where light-heeled ghosts, and visionary shades,
Beneath the wan cold moon."

ROBERT BLAIR

SORROWFUL REMEMBRANCE

ADONIS — *Adonis autumnalis*

"Th' unhappy fair Adonis likewise flowers,
Whom (once a youth) the Cyprian Queen deplores;
He, though transformed, has beauty still to move
Her admiration, and secure her love;
Since the same crimson blush the flower adorns
Which graced the youth, whose loss the goddess mourns."

RENÉ RAPIN

This dark crimson flower is said to have sprung from the blood of Adonis as it flowed from a death-wound caused by a boar; the anemone, in turn, is said to have sprung from the tears of Venus as she gazed on the bleeding corpse of the beautiful youth.

And in his blood that on the ground lay spilled
A purple flower sprang up, chequered with white,

WILLIAM SHAKESPEARE

SPLENDOUR or PATRIOTISM

Nasturtium (scarlet) – *Tropæolum*

Nasturtiums were first brought from Peru late in the sixteenth century. The name can be literally translated from the Latin as 'nose-twister' or 'nose-tormentor', referring to the plant's biting, pungent taste, reminiscent of watercress. Linnaeus devised the nasturtium's generic name, *Tropæolum*, from the Latin *Tropæum*, a trophy, because the helmet-shaped flowers and shield-like leaves conjured notions of the aftermath of battle, when Greeks and Romans would set up a tall trophy pole (the *tropæum*) and drape the armour and equipment of the vanquished foe on it as an emblem of victory. The flame flower, with its brilliant scarlet blooms, is one of the most beautiful and desirable of the species. Nasturtiums are also known as Indian cress and lark's heel, because "unto the backe-part (of the flowers) doth hang a taile or spurre, such as hath the Larkes heel" (Gerard). The flowers can be eaten in salads and the seeds can be substituted for capers.

STABILITY

CRESS — *Nasturtium officinale* and *Lepidium sativum*

Cress is one of the more ancient of salad plants. Its name derives from the Old English *cærse, cerse, cresse,* which means "to nibble or eat" Chaucer calls it *kers.* Gerard tells us that the Spartans were in the habit of eating cresses with their bread; this they did no doubt on account of an opinion held very generally among the ancients that those who ate cress became firm and resolute. Watercresses, according to astrologers, are herbs of the Moon. Watercress often occurs in place-names, such as Cresswell, Kerswell, "cress brook", "cress spring", signifying water nearby. Culpeper claimed that the bruised leaves or juice would free the face from blotches, spots and blemishes, when used as a lotion. Watercress has also been used as a specific in tuberculosis. Its active principles are said to be at their best when the plant is in flower. As a salad it promotes appetite.

"The cresses on the water and the Sorrell is at hand,"

STRENGTH
CEDAR – *Pinus cedrus*

Cedars are mentioned frequently in the Bible. The first tree was said to have been planted by Solomon, who later built a palace of Cedar on Lebanon – the Temple of Solomon. It was regarded as a sacred tree by Jews, and a noble one by Arabs, who called all the older trees saints and believed an evil fate would overtake anyone who injured them. Christ's cross was said to be composed of three woods – cypress, cedar and pine – symbolizing the Holy Trinity, with cedar representing God the Father. Virgil says that cedar wood was considered to be so durable that it was used for making images of the gods and effigies of ancestors. It was also used for fragrant torches and the Egyptians used it for the coffins of their dead as its rich smell drove away insects. The cedar is linked with notions of life, immortality and is generally considered to be a tree of good omen, protecting the good and overthrowing evil spirits.

TO SURMOUNT DIFFICULTIES
MISTLETOE – *Viscum album*

"Oaks, from whose branches,
Garlands of Spanish moss and of mystic Mistletoe flaunted,
Such as the Druids cut down with golden hatchets at Yule-tide."
HENRY WADSWORTH LONGFELLOW

Mistletoe has been used for centuries in Christmas decorations, although the one place it is not allowed is inside a church, because of its pagan history. It was a sacred plant to the Druids, who took care not to let it touch the ground and gave it to the people to fasten above their doorways to protect their houses from thunder, lightning and witchcraft. A parasitic plant, it was believed to hold the life of the host tree when the latter appeared dead in winter and has long been associated with fertility, from which the present-day custom of kissing under a sprig of mistletoe probably derives. Latterly, its associations are all to do with peace and goodwill and, since it stands in floral language for the truly Christian virtue of "surmounting all difficulties", perhaps the church should consider reinstating it.

SUPERSTITION

St John's Wort — *Hypericum perforatum*

*"St John's Wort, scaring from the midnight heath
The witch and goblin with its spicy breath."*

Superstition surrounds St John's wort. The plant has leaves marked with red, blood-like spots and is traditionally gathered on the eve of St John the Baptist's Day, 24 June, and hung in windows, over doors, or about the person as a charm against witchcraft, enchantment, storms and thunder. It is also known as *sol terrestris*, terrestrial sun, because of its bright yellow blossom and glittering golden stamens. Superstition states that all spirits of darkness vanish at the approach of the sun and St John's Day falls on the summer solstice, the old pagan festival of the sun. In the Isle of Man there is a saying that who-ever treads on it after sunset will be carried about on a fairy horse and not allowed to rest till sunrise. It is said to have the power to divine maidens' future husbands and reveal thieves. Dioscorides records its great reputation as a wound-herb.

SURPRISE

Betony — *Betonica*

"He has as many virtues as betony."

This proverb is common in Spain, where betony is still regarded for its efficacy in curing many complaints. It can, however, promote a kind of intoxication, which causes the patient to commit all kinds of extravagances, and the leaves, when dried and powdered into the form of snuff, produce immoderate sneezing - hence its meaning. Clare called it the "Medicinal Betony", and Turner, in his *Brittish Physician* — 1687 wrote: "It would seem a miracle to tell what experience I had of it. This herb is hot and dry, almost to the second degree, a plant of Jupiter in Aries, and is appropriated to the head and eyes, for the infirmities whereof it is excellent, as also for the breast and lungs; being boiled in milk, and drunk, it takes away pains in the head and eyes. Some write it will cure those that are possessed with devils, or frantic, being stamped and applied to the forehead."

SUSPICION

MUSHROOM – *Fungus*

"When the moon is at the full,
Mushrooms you may freely pull;
But when the moon is on the wane,
Wait ere you think to pluck again."

Because some species of mushrooms are poisonous, they have all been treated with caution and suspicion. In Wales the poisonous mushroom is called Bwyd Ellyllon, or "the meat of the goblins". Mushrooms and toadstools often grow in rings, springing up overnight, and the legend that these rings were formed by the feet of dancing fairies on the grass is an old one. In Indo-European mythology, the sun-hero is represented as sometimes hiding under a mushroom. Rich in vitamin D and calcium, mushrooms are the nearest thing to meat in the vegetable kingdom. To dream of gathering mushrooms indicates a lack of attachment on the part of a lover or consort.

TALENT

Pink (white) – *Dianthus*

"The Pink can no one justly slight,
The gardener's favourite flower;
He sets it now beneath the light,
Now shields it from its power."
Johann Wolfgang von Goethe

The pink is said to derive its name from the Dutch word *Pinkster*, Whitsuntide – the season at which the Whitsuntide gilliflower is in bloom. It is also known as lady's cushion, thrift, swift and cushings. Gerard observed them growing "in our pastures neere about London". In Italy the flower is held sacred to St Peter and 29 June – St Peter's Day – is known as the day of pinks in Bologna. The water distilled from pinks was said to be an excellent remedy for epilepsy, "but if a conserve be composed of it, it is the life and delight of the human race". A vinegar made of pinks was prized for its ability to stave off the plague.

TASTE

FUCHSIA (SCARLET) − *Fuchsia coccinea*

Sophisticated lady, party frock, swanley gem, mantilla, rose of Castile − we do not have to look further than the names given to some of the many varieties of this stunning flower to see where the meaning originated. Native to Mexico, Central and South America, the fuchsia was named in 1703 by Charles Plumier, a monk turned botanist, to honour the memory of the great German botanist Leonard Fuchs (1501-66). It is supposed to have been introduced to England in 1793 by the sailor son of a humble widow living in London. Thinking his mother would like it, he brought her a small plant home after a voyage to Chile and she put it on her windowsill, where it thrived. In the course of time she was persuaded to sell it to James Lee, an eminent nurseryman, for a reputed eighty golden guineas. Legend has it that the fuchsia was once a sweet smelling plant without flowers. Christ's blood was said to have fallen on it during the Crucifixion forming beautiful red and purple flowers that hung their heads in grief. In New Zealand, Maori women use the blue pollen of the *Fuchsia excorticata* for face adornment.

TEARS

HELENIUM − *Helenium*

"To me the meanest flower that blows can give
Thoughts that do often lie too deep for tears."
WILLIAM WORDSWORTH

The beautiful yellow flower of the helenium resembles small suns. It is said to have been named after Helen of Troy, whose beauty caused the Trojan war, and from whose tears it is said to have sprung, hence its meaning. Gerard wrote in his *Herbal*: "Some report that this plant tooke the name of *Helenium* from Helena, wife to Menelaus, who had her hands full of it when Paris stole her away into Phyrgia." *Helenium autumnale*, a species found in Canada and the eastern United States, is the parent of most garden cultivars, of which Moerheim beauty (bronze-red), Riverton beauty (yellow) and copper spray (copper-red) are examples. The common name − sneezeweed − refers to the use of the plant as errhine (promoting nasal discharge).

TEMPERANCE

AZALEA — *Azalea*

The Latin *azalea* comes from the Greek *azaleos*, meaning arid or dry, for this beautiful family of American plants grow naturally in dry soil only. The azalea is narcotic and poisonous in all its parts. Xenophon, in his narrative of the "Retreat of the Ten Thousand" from Asia after the death of Cyrus, tells how his soldiers became stupefied and delirious, as though drunk, after eating honey from Trebizond on the Black Sea. The baneful properties of the honey the men had eaten arose from the poisonous nature of the blossoms of the *Azalea pontica*, on which the bees had been foraging.

> *"I love a still conservatory*
> *That's full of giant breathless palms;*
> *Azaleas, clematis, and vines*
> *Whose quietness great trees becalms*
> *Filling the air with foliage,*
> *A curved and dreamy statuary."*
> WILLIAM TURNER

TEMPTATION

APPLE — *Malus domestica* or QUINCE — *Cydonia oblonga*

Ever since Eve offered Adam an apple from the Tree of Knowledge, the fruit has been associated with temptation. (Small boys have risked all punishment and "gone scrumping" ever since orchards were first planted.) The golden apples which Juno presented to Jupiter on the day of their nuptials were placed under the watchful care of a fearsome dragon in the garden of the Hesperides; but that did not prevent Hercules trying to procure some as one of his twelve labours. In popular tales of all countries, the apple is represented as the magical fruit *par excellence*, with mysterious, enchanting properties. Young girls would throw the peel over their heads to foretell whether they would marry or remain spinsters — if the peel remained whole, it was said to spell the initial of a coming sweetheart. Cider is made from apples and there are many intricate pastoral customs and wassailing songs connected with ensuring a good apple crop. The 'golden apples' of Virgil are said to be quinces.

THOUGHTS
YOU OCCUPY MY THOUGHTS
PANSY, OR HEART'S EASE – *Viola tricolor*

"Pray you love, remember,
And there are pansies, that's for thoughts."
WILLIAM SHAKESPEARE

Pansy, from the French *pensée*, a thought, and heart's ease, a name originally shared with wallflowers, are fairly mild names compared with such resounding appellations as: kiss-me-at-the-garden-gate, love-in-idleness, jump-up-and-kiss-me, meet-her-in-the-entry-kiss-her-in-the-buttery and three-faces-under-the-hood. Fable has it that the pansy was originally white but coloured purple by Cupid:

" – Yet marked I where the bolt of Cupid fell,
It fell upon a little Western flower.
Before, milk white, now purple with love's wound;
The maidens call it love-in-idleness."
WILLIAM SHAKESPEARE

TIMIDITY

MARVEL OF PERU – *Mirabilis jalapa*

"Rather the Maruell of the World than of Peru alone."
JOHN GERARD

The mirabilis was called marvel of Peru in reference to the plant's extremely abundant, highly-scented, gloriously coloured flowers, and to its country of origin. It arrived first in Spain from Peru in the sixteenth century and was made emblem of timidity because of its apparent shyness in displaying itself in the daytime. The blossoms seldom open before four o'clock in the afternoon, making it the four o'clock flower in many parts of the country; but then they remain open all night, encouraging the names belle de nuit, lady of the night and nightblower. Both in China and Japan the plant is used as a cosmetic – the flowers as rouge and the seeds as a white paste for the skin. In India the plant is used medicinally – the leaves are bruised and used as a poultice for boils and abscesses.

A TOKEN OF PATIENCE

OX-EYE DAISY — *Chrysanthemum leucanthemum*

"And at the laste there began anon
A lady for to sing right womanly
A bargaret in praising the Daisie:
For — as methought among her notes sweet,
She said, 'Si doucet est la Margarete.' "
GEOFFREY CHAUCER

The ox-eye daisy has many country names: butter-and-eggs, white moon daisy, lardy moon daisy and penny daisy. It is dedicated to Artemis, goddess of the moon, and to St John and Mary Magdalene. It grows in meadows and cornfields and was considered a divining flower by country people, who would patiently pluck the petals off while repeating "this year, next year, some time, never", to discover the date of their marriage. It was said to heal "burning ulcers, inflammation and the running of the eies", and from its connection with the moon, was thought efficacious in curing lunacy.

TRANQUILITY

STONECROP — *Sedum acre*

Like the houseleek, the stonecrop was thought to give protection — and thus tranquility — against thunder and lightning, and so was planted on the roofs of cottages and stables. It flourishes in its wild state on old stone or flint walls, rock, and on sandy ground. To chance upon an old wall in June or July,when the hundreds of blossoms are all open to the sunlight, is to understand in a flash why it is also called golden moss. It is known, too, as wall pepper and wall ginger (from the pungent taste of the leaves), Jack of the buttery, gold chain and prick madam. Herbalists valued the plant as a cure for ague and as an expeller of poisons. Culpeper wrote, "It is so harmless an herb that you can scarce use it amiss," and Linnaeus recommended it for scurvy and dropsy. It was used externally and, when boiled in beer, was considered good for pestilential fevers. It was used for all kinds of inflammations. Stonecrop is held by astrologers to be under the dominion of the moon.

TREACHERY

BILBERRY — *Vaccinium myrtillus*

The 'treachery' dates back to Greek mythology, when Myrtillus, son of Mercury, allowed himself to be bribed into pulling the linch-pin out of his master, Œnomaus's, chariot during a competition, Œnomaus was a skilled charioteer and proud of his prowess. He had a lovely daughter, Hippodamia, and insisted that all her suitors should compete with him in a chariot race. This proved to be his last race, for he was mortally wounded and implored Pelops to avenge him, which he did by throwing the treacherous Myrtillus into the sea. The waters bore his body back to the shore and Mercury changed it into this shrub. In Hawaii a species of bilberry called ohelo (*Vaccinium reticulatum*) springs up on decomposed lava. It has flame-coloured berries and was held sacred to Pélé, the goddess of the volcano. There may also be a touch of spite associated with the bilberry. In Shakespeare's *The Merry Wives of Windsor*, Pistol urges the elves and fairies to declare war on the servants of the surrounding houses:

> "Where fires thou find'st unraked and hearths unswept,
> There pinch the maids as blue as bilberry:
> Our radiant queen hates sluts and sluttery."

Also known as whortleberry, black whortles, whinberry, trackleberry, huckleberry, hurts, hurtleberry, blueberry, bleaberry and blaeberry, the bilberry, is often found growing on the seashore and has been used since the Middle Ages in medicine and cookery. The berries can be eaten fresh, when they have a slightly acid flavour, or cooked in soups, jams, preserves and pastry. Gerard wrote, 'The people of Cheshire do eate the black whortles in creame and milke as in these southern parts we eate strawberries.' Because of their rich juice, bilberries can be used with the least quantity of sugar in making jam. On the continent they are used to give a good colour to wine and in Britain at the beginning of the century they were used to provide a clear dark-blue or purple dye for wool. In Scotland it is known as blaeberry and its praises are sung in Northern ballads:

> "Will ye go, lassie, go to the braes of Balquhidder,
> Whare the Blaeberries grow 'mong the bonny blooming heather?"

TRUTH

BITTERSWEET NIGHTSHADE – *Solanum dulcamara*

"The first great work
Is, that yourself may to yourself be true."
WENTWORTH DILLON ROSCOMMON

The two tastes – bitter and sweet – combined in bittersweet night-shade led the Victorians to draw a parallel with truth, which is sometimes sweet, but frequently a bitter draught to swallow. John Gerard wrote of "Faire berries . . . very red when they be ripe, of a swete taste at the first, but after very unpleasant, of a strong savour; growing together in clusters like burnished corall." He recommended, "the juice is good for those that have fallen from high places and have thereby bruised or beaten, for it is thought to dissolve blood con-gealed or cluttered anywhere in the intrals and to heale the hurt places."

"The sting of a reproach is the truth of it."

166

UNANIMITY

Phlox – *Phlox*

"Come forth
In purple lights, till ev'ry hillock glows
As with the blushes of an evening sky."
Mark Akenside

Phlox was made emblem of unanimity because of the close grouping of its flowers. Pliny observed that the Greeks used a flower called phlox, meaning flame, in their garlands. They were introduced to Britain from North America in 1725 and grown by Miller in the botanic garden at Chelsea, where they were greatly admired for their brilliant colour. The Victorians used phlox a great deal in bouquets not only for their delightful fragrance but because they were also a symbol of sweet dreams and implied a proposal of marriage.

"Unanimous, as sons of one great sire."
John Milton

UNFORTUNATE LOVE
or WIDOWHOOD
SCABIOUS – *Scabiosa succisa*

This plant was named *scabiosa* by apothecaries because of its sup-posed ability to cure skin diseases such as scabies and leprosy. (This belief was based solely on the fact that the scabby external appearance of the plant somewhat resembled the disease it was supposed to cure!) Also known as sweet scabious, gypsy-rose, black-a-moor's beauty, devil's bit and mournful widow, it is used in the language of flowers to express widowhood, or "I have lost all" – because its dark purple corollas so nearly match the sable hue of widow's weeds it was considered an appropriate bouquet for those who mourn their deceased husband, and it used to be in great demand for funeral wreaths in Portugal and Brazil. The root of the plant is sup-posed to have been bitten off by the devil, who "bit the root in envy" because he did not want such a wholesome, useful plant to flourish and do good to mankind.

USELESSNESS
MEADOWSWEET – *Spirea ulmaria*

"The meadowsweet taunting high its showy wreath,
And sweet the quaking grasses hide beneath."
JOHN CLARE

Meadowsweet was made to signify uselessness because herbalists could find no medicinal use for it and because animals will not eat it. However, it was a great favourite as a strewing herb with Queen Elizabeth I and had another champion in Philip Miller, who considered its association with uselessness unjust: "Shall this sweet flower, so admirably advocated by a lady, any longer stand disgraced as the emblem of Uselessness, or will you not rather step forward and defend it as a Neglected Beauty, until some happier emblem is chosen?" Gerard tells us that the leaves "far excel all other strewing herbs, to deck up houses, to strew in chambers and halls for the smell thereof makes the heart merry and delighteth the senses."

VARIETY

CHINA ASTER — *Callistephus chinensis*

The China aster is so called not only because it came from that land, but also because its flowers resemble the many radii of a star. It is thought to have been introduced to Europe by a missionary, D'Incarville, who sent some seeds to the Jardin de Roi about 1730. It has been made emblem of variety because it is a plant showing a tremendous colour range, from white and soft yellow to pink, deep red, crimson and various shades of blue and mauve. There are single and double types, with large flowers in such strains as Ostrich Plume and Chrysanthemum-Flowered, and small bloooms in varieties such as Pompoms. The old English name of the aster is star-wort and in France is known as *La Reine Marguerite* . The aster is identified with the Amellus, of the Greek and Latin poets, and, according to Virgil, the altars of the gods were often adorned with wreaths of asters. The leaves, when burnt, had a reputation for driving away snakes. In Germany the aster is plucked like the common daisy to decide whether a lover's love is returned or not. The aster is considered to be a herb of Venus.

VICE

DARNEL — *Lolium temulentum*

"No fruitful crop the sickly fields return;
But oats and darnel choak the rising corn."
JOHN DRYDEN

Darnel was made emblem of vice because it used to grow alongside wheat, which it resembles in looks but differs totally from in quality. It is impossible to distinguish the good from the bad until harvest time and it was thus seen by farmers as a curse. They believed darnel to be sown by the devil at midnight and to be the tares of the gospel parable referred to in Matthew: "But while men slept, his enemy came and sowed tares among the wheat, and went his way. But when the blade was sprung up, and brought forth fruit, then appeared the tares also." If darnel and wheat are combined in flour and then baked, the bread will produce "drunken-like states of confused perceptions" when eaten. The Germans call it *Schwindel*, dizziness.

169

VICTORY

PALM — *Palmaceae*

"Be his the palm, who hath the conquest gained."

The palm tree is symbolic of victory, riches and generation – in Roman times, branches and garlands of palm were presented to winners of the games. The plant was also considered to be the emblem of light and was held sacred to Apollo; in the Christian church it is closely associated with the life of Jesus. As a child, He and His family found shelter and food beneath a palm tree and He made His triumphant entry into Jerusalem with a palm in His hand. It thus became the universal symbol of martyrdom and was depicted in early Italian paintings of the saints, as well as on the sculptured effigies of Christian heroes, including St Agnes, St Alban and St Pancras, the boy martyr. St Christopher was of such Herculean proportions that he is shown using a whole palm tree as his staff to steady himself while transporting travellers across the swollen river.

VIRTUE

MINT AND SAGE – *Mentha* and *Salvia officinalis*

"A little path of mintes full and fenill green."
GEOFFREY CHAUCER

Mint and sage are both highly regarded culinary and medicinal herbs. *Salvia* comes from the Latin *salvere*, "to be in good health", to save, or to heal. "Why should a man die whilst sage grows in his garden?" went an old Latin saying, and sage ale, wine and tea have been popular for centuries as tonics to help people live to a healthy old age. Menthe was a nymph beloved by Pluto, who was changed into the plant by the jealous Proserpine. For the Greeks and Romans, mint had many virtues and it was used as a bath scent, in cooking and in medicine. Aristotle started the belief that it was a powerful aphrodisiac and people were warned to take it in moderation. In the sixteenth century red garden mint, curled mint, spearmint, catmint and calamint were common garden plants.

VIVACITY

HOUSELEEK – *Sempervivum tectorum*

The houseleek has many popular names: Jupiter's beard, Jupiter's eye, bullock's eye, Thor's beard, thunderbeard and welcome-home-husband-though-never-so-drunk. The old Dutch name, *Donderbloem*, thunder-flower, derives from the popular belief that the plant was a preservative against thunder. Moreover, Sir Thomas Browne advised it should be planted on the roof of a house as "a defensative from lightning". It is considered unlucky to uproot the houseleek. It was once believed to suppress fevers given to children by witchcraft or sorcery and one Albartus Magnus used to rub his hands with the juice of the houseleek in order to to render them insensible to pain when he took a red-hot iron into his hands. In Italy, country girls were said to use it to predict their future husband – they gathered buds to represent their suitors and checked which had flowered most freely the following morning. According to astrologers, houseleek is a herb of Jupiter.

VOLUPTUOUSNESS

TUBEROSE – *Polyanthes tuberosa*

". . . The sweet tuberose,
The sweetest flower for scent that blows."
PERCY BYSSHE SHELLEY

The tuberose, so ostentatious in appearance and scent, was first introduced to Europe towards the end of the sixteenth century. A Dutch florist named La Cour then became passionately obsessed with it and achieved the first double-flowering variety, which made it highly sought after in aristocratic circles. In nineteenth-century Russia it was reserved exclusively for the gardens of the Imperial Court. The symbolism of the flower was keenly adhered to – blooms exchanged by lovers expressed strong mutual attraction. Famous for its fragrance, especially in the evening, the tuberose has a remarkable luminous quality and is known in Malay as the mistress of the night.

"The Tuberose, with her silvery light."
THOMAS MOORE

VORACIOUSNESS

LUPIN – *Lupinus*

"Where stalks of Lupines grew,
Th' ensuing season, in return, may bear
The bearded product of the golden year."
JOHN DRYDEN

The ancients named this plant *Lupinus*, from *lupus*, a wolf, on account of its voracious nature. It draws a great deal of the nourishment from the soil to feed itself, and because it is therefore full of goodness, makes an excellent manure for poor soil. The Romans cultivated lupins for food, soaking them first in hot water, or covering them with hot ashes, to take off the bitterness. Pliny says this diet imparted a fresh colour and a cheerful countenance. Eating lupins was also supposed to brighten the mind and quicken the imagination which is why Protogenes, a celebrated painter living on Rhodes about the year 328 BC, was said to have lived entirely on lupins and water for seven years.

VULGARITY

AFRICAN MARIGOLD – *Tagetes erecta*

"Open afresh your round of starry folds,
Ye ardent Marigolds!"
JOHN KEATS

In spite of its name, the African marigold is native to Mexico. "If the African marigold does not open its flowers in the morning around seven o'clock," says an old writer, "you may be sure it will rain that day, unless it thunders.' And Shakespeare speaks of: "The Marigold, that goes to bed with the sun/And with him rises weeping." According to Greek myth a girl named Caltha fell in love with the sun god, but was melted by his rays. In her place grew a solitary marigold. The flower has a reputation for ill luck in Germany, where young women are warned against using it to divine the future. It has acquired the rather damning meaning of vulgarity because, despite its looks, its odour is offensive: just as vulgar, showy people seek to impress with flashy clothes but little else, the African marigold has only its golden gaiety to recommend it.

WAR

Y ARROW – *Achillea millefolium*

Yarrow's association with war comes from Achilles, after whom the plant is named, who discovered its staunching powers when he applied it to his soldiers' wounds at the siege of Troy. Because of its antiseptic qualities, the plant has a reputation as a cure-all; it is also said to possess magical powers against enchantment. Its ability to stem the flow of blood has led to the local names soldier's woundwort, carpenter's weed and nosebleed. It was considered good for toothache, colds and rheumatism, and worn on the person for protection, or tied to babies' cradles to keep them from harm. The leaves produce a yellow dye. If eaten at a wedding, tradition had it that the couple would love each other for at least seven years. It has long been used in witches' incantations and for casting spells. It has also been used as snuff and was known as old man's pepper, because of its pungent foliage. To dream of yarrow means that you will soon hear of something that will give you great pleasure.

WARMTH or I BURN

Cᴀᴄᴛᴜs — *Cactus opuntia*

"The head and feet keep warm,
The rest will take no harm."
Fʀᴇɴᴄʜ Pʀᴏᴠᴇʀʙ

Most cacti are native to arid regions of America. For the Victorians they connoted warmth, and a burning heat linked discreetly to sexual desire. Many varieties have large, brilliantly coloured flowers or startlingly big edible fruits, which furthered the association with desire and fertility. The peyote cactus has been associated with drug addiction since pre-Columbian times; it is a well-known intoxicant, first used for ritual purposes by the Aztecs. The dried crowns, called mescal buttons and looking something like toadstools, contain the drug Mescaline. When chewed they induce hallucinations and a sense of well-being. (Aldous Huxley experimented with the drug when writing *Island* and *Heaven and Hell*.)

WISDOM

Mulberry Tree — *Morus alba*

*"And that old mulberry that shades the court
Has been my joy from very childhood up."*
Henry Kirke White

Pliny called the mulberry the wisest of trees because it is late in un-folding its leaves and so escapes the dangerous frost of early spring. The white mulberry was the trysting place of the lovers Thisbe and Pyramus, whose parents had forbidden their marriage. Ovid relates how Thisbe, arriving first at the tree, took shelter in a cave from a lioness. In her flight she dropped a veil, which the lioness smeared with blood. Pyramus found the bloody veil, concluded that his beloved Thisbe had been torn to pieces and, overcome with grief, fell on his sword. Thisbe then returned and, finding her lover dead, also threw herself upon the blade. With her last breath she prayed that her ashes should be mingled with her lover's in one urn, and that the fruit of the white mulberry tree should bear witness to their constancy by ever after assuming the colour of blood.

*"Hence Pyramus and Thisbe's mingled blood
On Mulberries their purple dye bestowed.
In Babylon the tale was told to prove
The fatal error of forbidden love."*
René Rapin

The large leaves support silkworms and, in China, where it is extensively cultivated, it is surrounded by superstition. In Burma the mulberry tree is held sacred and worshipped by hill tribes. The black mulberry, *Morus nigra* symbolizes survival. To dream of mulberries means good news. They denote marriage, many children and prosperity of all kinds. These dreams are particularly favourable to sailors and farmers.

*"He shall with vigour bear the summer's heat,
Who, after dinner, shall be sure to eat
His Mulberries, of blackest ripest dyes,
And gathered ere the morning sun arise."*
Philip Francis

WIT

RAGGED ROBIN — *Lychnis flos-cuculi*

"When St Barnabie bright smiles night and daie,
Poor Ragged Robin blossoms in the haie."
AN EARLY CALENDAR ENGLISH FLOWERS

Also known as cuckoo flower, meadow campion or meadow pink, ragged robin is so called because of the ragged appearance of the four cleft petals. "Robin" suggests the familiar, endearing cheerfulness of ragged robin in May and June, although some sources suggest that the plant is named after Robin Hood, whose adventures and wit continue to be celebrated. Ragged robin is dedicated to St Barnabas.

"This man I thought had been a lord among wits,
but I find he is only a wit among lords."
SAMUEL JOHNSON

YOU ARE WITHOUT PRETENSION

ROSE CAMPION — *Lychnis coronaria*

"But if to unjust things thou dost pretend,
Ere they begin, let thy pretensions end."
JOHN DENHAM

The simplicity and unassuming character of the rose campion has earned it this honourable meaning. The scarlet *Lychnis coronaria* is dedicated to St John the Baptist: following the Bible text which describes him as "a light to them which sit in darkness", the flame-coloured flower was said to be 'lighted up' for his festival on 24 June and is called *Candelabrum ingens*, great candlestick. The downy hairs which cover the stem and leaves were at one time used for lamp wicks, continuing the association with light. Henry Lyte an Elizabethan gardener and scholar, describes the flower as being of the colour of red-lead: "the flowers very pleasant and delectable to looke on, but without any pleasant sente or savour".

177

YOUR QUALITIES SURPASS YOUR CHARMS

MIGNONETTE – *Reseda odorata*

Romance surrounds the mignonette, or little darling, or *herbe d'amour*. During his Egyptian campaign Napoleon is supposed to have sent home seeds to Josephine, who grew the little yellow and white flowers as pot plants for the drawing rooms at Malmaison, thus starting a popular fashion which continued long into the nineteenth century. Then there is the tale of the Saxon noble, the Count of Walstheim, who transferred his affections from his beautiful heiress fiancée, Amelia von Nordburg, to her humble cousin Charlotte because the latter chose a modest spray of mignonette as her emblem during a party, while the coquettish Amelia had selected a rose. Recognizing that sincere affection and amiability had more worth than superficial beauty and flirtatiousness, he married Charlotte and added a branch of the sweet reseda to the ancient heraldic arms of his family, along with the motto: *Ses qualités surpassent ses charmes* (Your qualities surpass your charms).

YOUTH

FOXGLOVE – *Digitalis*

The foxglove, perhaps above all others, is the flower of the fairies: they were said to wear the flowers on their heads or as gloves and elves were thought to hide in the bell-shaped blooms. Fairies were also supposed to have given the corollas of the plant to foxes so that they could stalk poultry silently, or escape from man's snares. The plant's many local names reflect these magical associations: goblin's thimble, fairy cap, granny's gloves and lady's thimble. It is called foxglove because of the resemblance of its flowers to the fingers of a glove, and from its habit of growing on disturbed ground near the earths of foxes. Foxgloves were believed to give mysterious powers to those who held them and it was deemed unlucky to carry foxgloves on board ship. Despite being one of the most poisonous plants, its leaves contain digitalis, which was recognized by William Withering in 1799 as having a wide medicinal use and which is now the best-known and most widely-used medicine in treating heart disease.

YOU WILL CAUSE MY DEATH
HEMLOCK – *Conium maculatum*

"Root of Hemlock digg'd i' the dark."
WILLIAM SHAKESPEARE

The common hemlock is described by Dioscorides as a very evil, dangerous, hurtful and poisonous herb, "insomuch that whosoever taketh of it into his body dieth remediless, except the party drank some wine before the venom hath taken the heart". Socrates is said to have been poisoned by hemlock. In Russia hemlock is looked on as a satanic herb; in Germany it is regarded as a funereal plant, from infernal regions. In England, where it is often found growing among ruins and in waste places, it was said to be a favourite plant of witches, gathered by them for use in their potions and consequently considered a plant of ill omen.

"By the witches' tower,
Where Hellebore and Hemlock seem to weave
Round its dark vaults a melancholy bower
For spirits of the dead at night's enchanted hour."
THOMAS CAMPBELL

ZEALOUSNESS
ELDER – *Sambucus*

Elder trees are certainly zealous – they flourish anywhere in reasonably good soil. They are widely found in gardens as they were highly respected and cherished as magical trees, an infallible protection against evil, including witches and lightning. The wood, leaves, flowers and berries all had their household uses, and all parts had safe, beneficial medicinal properties. John Evelyn wrote: "If the medicinal properties of its leaves, bark and berries were fully known, I cannot tell what our countryman could ail for which he might not fetch a remedy from every hedge, either for sickness, or wounds." Hippocrates prescribed it for illness, the Romans made their hair-dye from its berries and Pliny said that the best flues and pipes were those made from elder trees which had grown where no cock-crows could be heard.

ZEST

L E M O N — *Citrus limon*

"The Median fields rich citron fruit produce
Tho' harsh the taste, and clammy be the juice,
Blest antidote! which when in evil hour,
The step-dame mixes herbs of pois'nous pow'r
And crowns the bowl with many a mutter'd spell
Will from the veins the direful draught expel,
Large is the trunk, and laurel-like its frame,
And 'twere a laurel, were its scent the same.
Its lasting leaf each roaring blast defies,
Tenacious of the stem its flow'rets rise;
Hence a more wholesome breath the Medes receive,
And of their sores the lab'ring lungs relieve."

VIRGIL

The tangy sharpness of lemons and the tales of adventures and exploration which lie behind their introduction to Europe and America has made them emblematic of zest. Lemons probably reached Europe overland from the East by the old caravan trade routes through Persia. Christopher Columbus is credited with taking seeds of lemons, citron and bitter oranges to the New World during his second voyage of discovery.

"Bear me, Pomona,
To where the lemon and the piercing lime
With the deep orange, glowing through the green,
Their lighter glories blend."

Theophrastus, describing the fruits around 300 BC, said they were considered an antidote to poison and, according to Athenaeus, certain notorious criminals, who had been condemned to be destroyed by serpents, saved their lives by eating citrons.

"Into an oval form the citrons rolled
Beneath thick coats their juicy pulp enfold;
From some the palate feels a poignant smart,
Which though they wound the tongue yet heal the heart."

RENÉ RAPIN

INDEX

(And Full List of Flowers and Their Meanings)

Entries in bold type appear in the book on the page numbers listed

The Innocence of Early Youth promotes Joy
Innocence and Purity are here represented by the daisies and the Star of Bethlehem;
Early Youth by primroses and Mirth and Joy by the yellow crocus and wood sorrel.

INDEX

INDEX

188

THE OFFICIAL STATE FLOWERS OF THE U.S.A.

The emblematic flower of each of the United States is listed below. In 1986 President Ronald Reagan signed Proclamation 5574, which officially recognized the rose as the national floral emblem of the United States.

American Beauty Rose – District of Columbia
Apple Blossom – Arkansas, Michigan
Big Rhododendron – West Virginia
Bitterroot – Montana
Black-Eyed Susan – Maryland
Bluebonnet – Texas
Blue Iris – Tennessee
Camellia – Alabama
Cherokee Rose – Georgia
Dogwood – Virginia, North Carolina
Forget-Me-Not – Alaska
Golden Poppy – California
Goldenrod – Kentucky, Nebraska
Hawthorn – Missouri
Indian Paintbrush – Wyoming
Lady's Slipper – Minnesota
Magnolia – Louisiana, Mississippi
Mayflower (or Arbutus) – Massachusetts
Mistletoe – Oklahoma
Mountain Laurel – Connecticut, Pennsylvania
Native Sunflower – Kansas
Native Violet – Illinois

Orange Blossom – Florida
Oregon Grape – Oregon
Pasque Flower – South Dakota
Peach Blossom – Delaware
Peony – Indiana
Purple Lilac – New Hampshire
Purple Violet – New Jersey
Red Clover – Vermont
Rocky Mountain Columbine – Colorado
Rose – New York
Sagebrush – Nevada
Saguaro Cactus Blossom – Arizona
Scarlet Carnation – Ohio
Sego Lily – Utah
Syringa – Idaho
Violet – Rhode Island
Western Rhododendron – Washington
White Pine Cone and Tassel – Maine
Wild Prairie Rose – North Dakota
Wild Rose – Iowa
Wood Violet – Wisconsin
Yellow Hibiscus – Hawaii
Yellow Jessamine – South Carolina
Yucca – New Mexico

A WHO'S WHO OF HERBALISTS AND BOTANICAL WRITERS

WILLIAM BULLEIN (d. 1576) English physician, born early in the reign of Henry VIII, author of *Book of Simples*, 1562.

COLUMELLA, Lucius Junius Moderatus (c.40 AD) Latin writer on gardening and agriculture who lived mostly in Rome at the time of Nero.

NICHOLAS CULPEPER (1616-1654) Best-selling English writer on astrology and medicine, who died aged 38 of consumption brought on by overwork.

DIOSCORIDES, Pedanius (1st century) A Greek physician, living in the reign of Nero, author of an important five volume work, *De Materia Medica*.

JOHN EVELYN (1620-1706) English author and diarist, with a lively and scientific interest in gardening and forestry. Author of *Terra*; 1676.

JOHN GERARD (1545-1612) English botanist. Educated as a surgeon, he established a wonderful physic garden at Holborn. Chiefly famous for his *Herball or General Historie of Plants*, 1597.

CARL LINNAEUS (1707-1778) Swedish botanist. He was the first to classify plants according to species, orders and sub-kingdoms.

PHILIP MILLER (1681-1771) British botanist, curator of the physic garden at Chelsea and author of *The Gardener's Dictionary*, 1724.

JOHN PARKINSON (1567-1650) English apothecary and herbalist. Had a garden at Long Acre 'well stocked with rarities' and was apothecary to King James I. Author of *Paradisus Terrestris*, 1629.

PLINY The Elder (AD 23-79) Roman soldier and author of *Naturalis Historia*, a wide ranging encyclopaedic 37 volume work.

WILLIAM SALMON (1644-1713) English apothecary. Controversial in his time. Author of *Practical Physick*, 1692.

JOHN TRADESCANT (d. 1637) English traveller, naturalist and royal gardener, established a physic garden and museum (Tradescant's Ark) at Lambeth.

THOMAS TUSSER (1524?-1580) English agricultural writer and poet. Author of a *Hundreth Good Pointes of Husbandrie*, 1557.

AUTHOR'S NOTE

Lest any reader should be tempted by the quotes I have reproduced from old herbalists recommending various plants as medicinal remedies, let me recommend that they should be treated with circumspection. Many plants are poisonous.

I believe all my sources are out of copyright, however, I have ranged wide in researching this book and if I have inadvertently failed to credit an elusive author I offer my apologies.